8.6·05

Remember
Laughter

Remember Laughter

A Life of
James Thurber

NEIL A. GRAUER

University of Nebraska Press
Lincoln and London

Grateful acknowledgment is made to The Ohio State
University Libraries, Rare Books and Manuscripts, for
supplying the photographs and to Rosemary Thurber
for permission to use them. "The Seal in the Bedroom" © 1932, 1960 James Thurber. From *The Seal
in the Bedroom,* published by Harper & Row.
"Thurber and His Circle" © 1962 Helen Thurber.
© 1990 Rosemary A. Thurber. From *Credos and
Curios,* published by Harper. "He's having all his
books . . ." © 1966. Originally published in *The New
Yorker* with another caption. From *Thurber &
Company,* published by Harper & Row. Remaining
drawings © 1943 James Thurber. © 1971 Helen
Thurber and Rosemary A. Thurber. From *Men,
Women and Dogs,* published by Harcourt Brace
Jovanovich, Inc. © 1994 by the University
of Nebraska Press. All rights reserved. Manufactured
in the United States of America. ♾ The paper in this
book meets the minimum requirements of American
National Standard for Information Sciences –
Permanence of Paper for Printed Library Materials,
ANSI Z39.48-1984. Third cloth printing: 1995
First paperback printing: 1995
Most recent printing indicated by last digit below:
10 9 8 7 6 5 4 3 2 1
Library of Congress Cataloging in Publication Data.
Grauer, Neil A. Remember laughter: a life of James
Thurber / Neil A. Grauer. p. cm. Includes
bibliographical references (p.) and index.
ISBN 0-8032-2155-X (cl.) ISBN 0-8032-7056-9 (pbk.)
1. Thurber, James, 1894–1961 – Biography. 2.
Humorists, American – 20th century – Biography. I.
Title. PS3539.H94Z68 1995 818'.5209 – dc20 [B]
94-2945 CIP

"Remember laughter.
You'll need it even in
the blessed isles of
Ever After."

James Thurber
The 13 Clocks

For

Robert D. Chessin
Thomas A. Cole
Charles S. Fax and
James R. Ledley

*a band
of brothers*

Contents

Illustrations

Acknowledgments

Those who knew James Thurber in life, and others who now are preserving his legacy, have assisted me in gathering material for this book, putting it in perspective, and placing it between these covers. Foremost among them is Rosemary Thurber, whose devotion to her father's memory is enhanced by her wise assessments and generosity of spirit. Those who knew Thurber and graciously agreed to be interviewed about him include the late William L. Shirer, his oldest friend; Roger Angell and Philip Hamburger, Thurber's *New Yorker* colleagues; Al Hirschfeld, who has known everyone in New York's theatrical, artistic, and literary world for more than six decades and immortalized them in line like no one else; Heywood Hale Broun, who has known almost as many folks as Hirschfeld and whose insights are equally sharp; and Art Buchwald, whose acquaintance with Thurber was brief but whose understanding of humor is boundless.

Also lending generous assistance were Russell Baker, whose knowledge of humor is as capacious as Buchwald's; John Updike; Garrison Keillor; Steve Allen and Audrey Meadows; Donn F. Vickers and Michael J. Rosen of The Thurber House in Columbus, Ohio; Geoff Smith of the Thurber Collection at Ohio State University, and Elva Griffith of the Rare Books and Manuscripts Room of the Ohio State University Libraries; Green Lawn Cemetery in Columbus; Linda Zycherman of Stoneledge, Inc.; Linda Kulman of *The New Yorker;* David Thomas, the last editor of *Punch,* and the staff of the Enoch Pratt Free

Library in Baltimore; Diane MacEachern, Maria Rodriguez, and my colleagues at Vanguard Communications in Washington, D.C.

Even the most reclusive writers require the encouragement of friends. Of those who gave me unstinting support, none did more yeoman service than John Halperin, Centennial Professor of English at Vanderbilt University, who reviewed the entire manuscript and offered the insights and suggestions that only a fellow author could provide.

As another friend who has written some books once told me, acknowledgments such as these enable an author to shake hands with his friends in print. I have many indulgent, helpful, and steadfast friends, but those I owe an especially grateful, ink-stained handclasp, for this book and for other things, are my father, Dr. William S. Grauer, and his wife, Jane, my brother, Tony, his wife, Helene, and daughters Myndi and Robyn, John and Anne Bainbridge, James and Mary Bready, Neil L. Buttner, Thomas and Sue Connor, Christopher and Rebecca Corbett, Joseph and Ozzie Cowan, Alice and Lou D'Angelo, Marc and Alice Davis, Caleb, Mary Jo, Zooey, and Emily Deschanel, Daniel Mark Epstein, Robert and Elise Erlandson, John and Elaine Fairhall, Stan and Bailey Fine, Graeme and Ronda Fox, Charles and Chris Goodell, Hugh and Janet Graham, Robert and Ginny Green, Henry Greenberg and Ann LoLordo, George and Barbara Hanst, Mark and Pat Heaney, Richard and Ellen Hollander, David M. Howland, Jr., Geoff and Sue Huntting, Rob and Sue Kasper, Mitch and Sue Kearney, John and Carol Kelly, Hugh and Mary Anne Kenner, Quint E. Kessenich, Kevin Kilner, Richard and Catherine Macksey, Les and Julie Matthews, H. Downman and Helen McCarty, Robert N. Miller IV, Joseph and JoAnn Murphy, Kenneth and Nancy Niman, Pat and Gale O'Connor, Michael Patterson, Steve and Sheila Sachs, Gilbert Sandler, Mark and Jeanne Shriver, Kevin and Dottie Simpson, Gus and Katherine Slotman, Sylvia and the late Normand Stulman, Glen and Chris Thomas, Paul and Elizabeth Valentine, Brooke E. White, and Jack and Byrd Wood.

Introduction

On a cold February day in 1991, three employees of Stoneledge, Inc., a fine arts conservation and restoration company in Wharton, New Jersey, used manual saws to remove three sections of a dingy wall from the longtime office of *The New Yorker* magazine at 25 West 43rd Street in Manhattan. As much delicacy as possible was used in this unusual surgery. Special cradles had been built to hold the pieces of gypsum block wall, each of which was seven inches thick and weighed over 100 pounds. Thick, custom-designed aluminum frames were fitted around the irregularly shaped pieces, which then were covered with protective safety glass and carefully inserted into another wall, in *The New Yorker*'s new office at 20 West 43rd Street, right across the way.[1]

This elaborate procedure, overseen by experts in archaeology and artifact preservation, was performed in order to save three large pencil sketches scrawled on the wall long ago by James Thurber. If you believe in ghosts, as Thurber did, then it is a reasonable supposition that his lanky, rumpled shade was hovering nearby, smiling with quiet satisfaction. By such an enshrinement of these wispy remnants of his genius, Thurber's elevation as an icon – something he had feared might never occur – now seems complete.

Humorous writing and drawing discourage veneration. A half-century ago, E. B. White, Thurber's mentor and colleague at *The New Yorker,* wrote, "The world likes humor, but treats it patronizingly.

It decorates its serious artists with laurel, and its wags with Brussels sprouts." White noted that Mark Twain once described his sobering scan of a "mortuary volume" of works by some long-forgotten contemporaries and reflected on how so little of what they had written remained funny. "Humor is only a fragrance, a decoration," Twain wrote. "Often it is merely an odd trick of speech and of spelling . . . and presently the fashion passes and fame along with it. . . . Humor must not professedly teach, and must not professedly preach, but it must do both if it would live forever." Then Twain added dolefully: "By forever, I mean thirty years." [2]

What is remarkable about Thurber's work is that so many of his books meet Twain's test for durability and remain in print three decades after his death in 1961. Of the twenty-five volumes Thurber published during his lifetime, twenty or so remain readily available – some more than a half-century after their original publication. That is an extraordinary testimonial to the enduring quality of his literary and artistic creations. What he wrote and drew still speaks to many of us and most likely will address our descendants.

Perhaps an equally remarkable aspect of the enduring quality of Thurber's work has been its continuing popularity despite the undeniable misogynist tinge to much of his writing, and the widely circulated, uncontested tales of his private misanthropy. He was not the always-lovable boon companion that his idol Robert Benchley had been, and unlike those who may once have run afoul of Mark Twain in full eruption, many of the people Thurber offended lived long after him. Some of them live still.

Now that more than thirty years have passed since Thurber's death and a century since his birth, the years have diminished the impact of his foibles and further enhanced the stature of his creations, confirming their timelessness and enabling us to place them in dispassionate perspective.

Thurber's sly, incisive, sometimes pointedly bittersweet or haunting stories and cartoons illuminate themes with which every reader can identify. In "The Secret Life of Walter Mitty," one of the most popular short stories of this century, Thurber created a character whose name has become not only a byword but also an emblem of our time: a man who escapes from the mundane anxieties of modern life (as well as his badgering wife) by taking refuge in daydreams. And as a cartoonist, Thurber was wholly original, without artistic forebear or issue. In the history of American comic art, no cartoonist can be cited as Thurber's inspiration, and none can be said to have been influenced by his style. Predecessors may have drawn simple, primitive figures, but these were not genuine precursors to Thurber's unique men, women, and dogs; and no artist since has dared emulate his drawings, with their strange yet wonderful blend of childlike draftsmanship and sophisticated wit.*

In a self-mocking but insightful analysis of his drawings, Thurber wrote that when classifying the creative origins of his cartoons, he found that they could be placed "into five separate and indistinct categories."[3] First there was the Unconscious or Stream of Nervousness category, represented by, among others, the drawing of a worried-looking man saying to a clearly distraught woman, "With you I have known peace, Lida, and now you say you're going crazy." Then Thurber discerned a Purely Accidental and Haphazard category, which included

---

*That isn't to say Thurber's cartoons have had no impact whatsoever on would-be artists. In May 1993, Matt Groening, creator of "The Simpsons," told *The Washington Post* that as a child he "took great comfort in the work of James Thurber, the only cartoonist that draws worse than I ever did."

his renowned "Seal in the Bedroom" and "Lady on the Bookcase" cartoons, both the result, he insisted, of inept draftsmanship run amok. He said this also could be called the "Deliberate Accident or Conditional Mistake" category. A third grouping, Category No. 3, he solemnly described as "Perhaps a variant of Category No. 2; indeed they may even be identical." He called the fourth category "Contributed Idea," a group of drawings for which somebody else came up with the situation or caption but deemed him more suited to executing it. Among these was his famous drawing of one fencer neatly slicing off the head of another, saying simply, "Touché!"

The final grouping, Thurber wrote, could be called "the Intentional or Thought-Up category," featuring drawings for which the idea "just came to me and I sat down and made a sketch to fit the prepared caption." This group would include the cartoon of a Thurber family: disconsolate husband slumped in a chair and patting the head of the family dog, a nondescript little boy, an annoyed wife, and a blank-faced daughter with a bow in her hair, to whom the mother is saying, "Well, I'm disenchanted, too. We're all disenchanted." Thurber wrote that perhaps an "Outside Force" played a part in this cartoon's creation. "I may have heard a husband say to his wife, on the street or at a party, 'I'm disenchanted,'" and such a chance remark elicited the cartoon. He could not be certain if that was so.[4]

The unexplained – indeed, inexplicable – origins of Thurber's cartoon ideas epitomizes as forcefully as anything the mysterious nature of creativity; and the timeless humor in them exemplifies his own special genius.

As spontaneous as Thurber's drawings were, his writing was infinitely labored. He told one interviewer that he rarely had a clear idea of what he wanted to write when he began a piece, just a general concept of "people and a situation." "Then I fool around – writing and rewriting until the stuff jells."[5] He scorned outlines, telling another interviewer, "I don't believe the writer should know too much where he's going. If he does, he runs into old man blueprint."[6]

Thurber estimated that his first draft for most stories ran only 500 to 1,500 words, and he readily confessed that it tended to be terrible: "The first or second draft of everything I write reads as if it was turned out by a charwoman." His wife Helen, he said, often dismissed his initial efforts as "high-school stuff." He would assure her, "Wait until the seventh draft, it'll work out all right."[7] He claimed to have rewritten some stories fifteen complete times before he was satisfied, if he ever was entirely pleased with a piece. He hated to surrender an article to his editors, believing that the longer he worked on it – trimming, expanding, refining, or just thinking about it – the better it would be.[8]

This elaborate labor produced elegantly simple prose, "jewels of English writing," as Russell Baker has observed.[9] Despite Thurber's claim that he did not know where he was headed when he began a piece, his old friend Stephen Vincent Benét, the poet, believed that Thurber knew the route by which he would get there: Benét once characterized the essence of Thurber's humor as a conscious and definite distortion of reality.[10]

Perhaps the most impressive – and poignant – fact about Thurber's writing is that he did some of his finest work after he went blind in the early 1940s. Living the last twenty years of his life in a soft, milky mist of diffuse light, Thurber demonstrated extraordinary courage and the scope of his genius by becoming, as E. B. White put it, an ear-writer rather than an eye-writer. Slowly, deliberately, he composed sentences, paragraphs, stories, and books in his head, then used his prodigious memory to retain, refine, and dictate them. Despite his disability, bouts of severe depression, and other enervating illnesses, Thurber published more books after he had gone blind than before, and the sound of words, the tricks he could play with them, became central to his humor, rather than the comical situations or personalities he could describe. Indeed, his descriptions concentrated increasingly on the aural, not the visual.

Thurber called himself an "old word man" from the very beginning of his career,[11] and some of the best stories he wrote before he went blind dealt with how confusion and even chaos can overwhelm us when a word is misspoken or misunderstood; how, for example, the entire population of Columbus, Ohio, fled in a frenzy as soldiers sought to assure them that "the dam has *not* broken," but the "stampeders thought the soldiers were bellowing 'the dam has now broken!' thus setting an official seal of authentication on the calamity."[12]

If words were the beginning for Thurber, as blindness enveloped him they gradually became an end in themselves, a source of tragedy as well as humor. In "The Whip-Poor-Will," the incessant chirping of a bird outside a bedroom window unhinges the already unstable protagonist, Kinstrey, as the bird's rhythmic twitter is transformed in his mind into words of mayhem and murder: "whip-poor-will" becomes "whip him now" and "cut your throat." When Thurber began writing fairy tales in 1943, after he lost his sight, his preoccupation with sound grew more pronounced. Language became not just a key element of the stories – as it would be in the work of any fine writer – but in many respects the subject of the stories themselves. As Catherine McGehee Kenney has observed, onomatopoeia, neologisms, alliteration, allusions, anagrams, and riddles abound in these supposed children's books.[13] They are the works of a writer who is as enthralled by the sound of words as by their sense. Consider his account in *The White Deer* of a party of hunters in search of game: "Twenty hoofs thundered hotly through a haunted hollow of spectral sycamores hung with lighted lanterns and past a turquoise tarn and along an avenue of asphodel that turned and twisted down a dark descent which led at last to a pale and perilous plain." [14]

As Kenney also notes, the instructions given to one of the questing princes in *The White Deer* contain allusions to popular music, a singer, and even politicians. Prince Gallow is told he will find the Seven-Headed Dragon of Dragore, which he must slay, by going "down and down, round and round, through the moaning Grove of Artanis," where lurk "the dreadful Tarcomed" and "the surly Nacilbuper." One need only reverse the spelling of "Nacilbuper," "Tarcomed," and "Artanis" to get Republican, Democrat, and Sinatra, who in the old Coconut Grove nightclub may have crooned the lyric from "That Old Black Magic": "Down and down I go, round and round I go, / In a spin, love is the spin I'm in, / Under that old black magic called love." The Prince, on his own mission for love, is told that when he emerges from the Grove of Artanis, he must turn "to the right and follow a little white light" – another Thurber allusion to a song lyric, the one providing directions to "My Blue Heaven." [15]

At the end of his career, with *The Wonderful O*, a children's story about the havoc that ensues when the letter O is banished from the language, Thurber could echo the remark of Samuel Beckett: "Words are all we have." [16]

Thurber was scornful of the word *genius* when it was applied to himself. He testily wrote to friends in 1950: "I was a reporter without enough genius to get off newspapers and make more than forty a week until I was thirty-two. Anybody with the slightest critical ability knows that a genius would not have to slave over his prose so long, or over his drawings so little." [17]

That crotchety self-assessment aside, Thurber knew that genius is in the inspiration as much as the execution, and the breadth of his work –

the short stories, essays, parodies, fables, fantasies, plays, biographical sketches, and cartoons – amply confirms the astonishing variety of his imagination and creativity.

Thurber drew, in prose and pictures, exquisite vignettes of idiosyncrasy and domestic turmoil; he delineated enchanting fantasies and pungent fables; he made of his personal troubles and torment a humorous world that readers decades hence can enjoy. As has been written of Dickens, so it also can be said of Thurber: part of his genius was "to transform this great sadness into uproarious comedy." [18] His work endures because it is universal. It captures conflicts, anxieties, and longings inherent in us all.

Remember
Laughter

Jamie and the Seairoplane

If heredity is destiny, then James Thurber probably was fated to be a bit odd, although not necessarily funny. (His two brothers were merely odd.)

Thurber's maternal great-grandfather, Jacob Fisher, was a huge blacksmith renowned for stern religious and political beliefs, fiercely defended with his fists. Nevertheless, while he fought like a demon in support of Methodism and in opposition to Andrew Jackson, he also was known to treat the wounds of his vanquished foes and to harbor no enduring animosity toward them. He was a man of immense strength and singularity of purpose who sometimes picked up a horse to move it from one place to another, rather than go to the trouble of leading it around.[1]

Jacob Fisher fathered thirteen children, among whom was William M. Fisher, Thurber's maternal grandfather. Eager whenever traveling to announce loudly in public, "I am William M. Fisher, of Columbus, Ohio," he liked to walk down the street with a rose clamped between his gold-capped teeth and to be photographed whenever possible, in an age when photography was rare. One full-length photo portrait, showing Fisher in his overcoat and derby hat and carrying a satchel, hung in his living room as a memento of the last-minute cancellation of a journey on a small excursion boat that subsequently sank with all on board. Thurber later would attribute this monumental display of ego and some of his grandfather's other quirks to the title character in his short story "The Luck of Jad Peters."

William Fisher liked to mimic, if not exactly emulate, his father's combativeness by swinging at opponents without actually hitting them. When in time he became the family patriarch, he would enjoin his Thurber grandsons to ignore any cuts or bruises by shouting at them, "Show your Fisher, boy, show your Fisher!" Thurber's wife thought her grandfather-in-law had a tenuous grasp on sanity.[2]

A prosperous wholesaler of fruits and vegetables who could precisely identify almost a thousand varieties of apples, the pugnacious William M. Fisher somehow attracted a complete opposite and married a gentle, generous young woman named Katherine Matheny Taylor. Her family tree had its own quirky offshoots, mostly oddball aunts whose bizarre traits would later provide their grandnephew James with the grist for a seemingly inexhaustible supply of anecdotes about eccentric relatives. One aunt smoked plugs of chewing tobacco in a pipe, another had recurring dreams in which she gave birth to Chinese, Indian, Mexican, and African twins, and a third once labored futilely over the mechanism of a broken cream separator only to shock her prim household by dropping all vestiges of Victorian gentility and finally exclaiming, "Why doesn't somebody take this goddam thing away from me?"[3]

The first of William and Katherine Fisher's six children was Thurber's mother, Mary Agnes Fisher, born in 1866 and known to all as "Mame." She carried on — and came to embody — the tradition of Fisher-Thurber eccentricity. A free spirit who longed for a career on the stage, she was thwarted once in an attempt to run away and become an actress. Instead, she took to acting out elaborate practical jokes at home and around Columbus, wringing at least a modicum of fame from within the confines of her hometown.[4] Toward the end of his life, Thurber would recall his mother as "a born comedienne," to whom he owed "practically everything." She was, he felt, "one of the finest comic talents I think I've ever known."[5] Among other escapades, she once attended a faith healer's revival in a wheelchair, pretending to be a cripple, then jumped up to howl hosannas and proclaim herself cured. On another occasion, Thurber recalled in "Lavender with a Difference," his mother "distressed a couple of stately guests in her father's home by descending the front stairs in her dressing gown, her hair tumbling and her eyes staring, to announce that she had escaped from the attic, where she was kept because of her ardent and hapless love for Mr. Briscoe, the postman."[6]

Perhaps of equal displeasure to her father was the genuine love Mame Fisher developed for Charles Leander Thurber, a thoroughly unprepossessing political clerk with a knack for aligning himself with losing candidates.

Charles Thurber's father, Leander, was a native of New England who went west to dig for gold in California but never got beyond Indianapolis, Indiana, where he met and married Sarah Hull. Along with Sarah came her unmarried sister, who was reputed in some family gossip to be the actual mother of the infant Charles, born in 1867. No proof ever surfaced of the supposed illegitimacy of Thurber's father, although Mame Thurber tried to find out if it was true years after her husband's death.[7]

Not too long after Charles Thurber was born, his father was tossed from a horse and killed. As a schoolteacher, Sarah Thurber struggled to support her son and her now chronically ill sister, but the strain broke her physically and mentally. Young Charles was able to complete only the eighth grade before having to go to work full-time to support his ailing mother and aunt.

Although the idea of a career on the stage appealed to him, which

3

in due course partly accounted for the appeal he found in the irrepressible Mame Fisher, neither theatrics nor the law, to which he also was
attracted, were likely professions for a poor, sparsely educated youth.
Instead, with his extraordinary memory – a trait he shared with Mame
Fisher and passed on to his son James – and his attention to meticulous
language and penmanship, Charles Thurber obtained the first of many
clerical jobs that would constitute his career. The blend of legal and
theatrical skills in politics particularly intrigued him, so he eventually
found work as a political factotum for various elected officials.

Having met Mame Fisher on a trip to Columbus in 1884, when he
was seventeen, Charles Thurber courted her by mail and periodic visits
for the next eight years. They finally were married in 1892 in a church
not far from William Fisher's mansion and settled in Columbus. The
prominent, aggressive Fisher clan rapidly enveloped the nondescript
Charlie Thurber, who moved through the ranks of political clerkdom
to become a staff aide to two Ohio governors, secretary to the State Republican Executive Committee, and secretary to the mayor of Columbus. He seemed happiest, however, when honing his skills as a solver
of newspaper puzzle contests. His son James recalled in "Gentleman
from Indiana" that in a half-century as a tireless contestant, Charles
Thurber "won a trip to the St. Louis World's Fair, a diamond ring, a
victrola, two hundred dollars' worth of records, and many cash prizes,
the largest, fifteen hundred dollars, as first prize in a proverb contest."
He was woefully inept with anything mechanical. Once, while trying
to fix the lock on his sons' small rabbit pen, he managed to lock himself inside with thirteen guinea pigs and six Belgian hares. But he also
had a sensitive, literary side and knew most of James Whitcomb Riley's
poems by heart.[8]

The newlywed Thurbers' first son, William Fisher Thurber, was born
in 1893. His proud grandfather soon bought the young parents their

4

own home at 251 Parsons Avenue, where on December 8, 1894 – "on a night of wild portent and high wind" – James Grover Thurber was born. He was named for James Grover, the town's first librarian, a Methodist minister, and a close friend of Grandfather Fisher. "I often thank our Heavenly Father that it was the Reverend James Grover, and not another friend of the family, the Reverend Noah Good, to whom the Fishers were so deeply devoted," Thurber wrote. His family always called him Jamie. In 1896, the Thurber family welcomed the arrival of Robert, the third and final son.[9]

By that time, Charles Thurber was Correspondence Clerk in the office of Ohio Governor Asa S. Bushnell, an important-sounding but meagerly paid position. In 1900, the fortunes of politics diminished the Thurber family's circumstances even more when Governor Bushnell was booted from office. A good six months went by before Charles Thurber secured new employment as secretary to an Ohio congressman, and the family had to sell its Columbus home and move to Washington, D.C.

It was at their rented summer residence in Falls Church, Virginia, just outside Washington, that six-year-old Jamie Thurber fell victim to an accident that haunted him – and all of his family – for the rest of his life. One hot Sunday afternoon in 1901, while playing with home-made bows and arrows, Jamie was serving as the target in an apple-less version of William Tell when his older brother, William, accidentally shot an arrow into his left eye. Charles Thurber was away on a fishing trip and Mame Thurber, then flirting with Christian Science, hesitated about seeking medical treatment. Eventually she compromised by taking Jamie to an inept general practitioner, not a specialist, who wrongly told her to leave the blinded eye in place. The failure to remove the damaged, useless eye led to "sympathetic ophthalmia," an inflammation of the undamaged eye caused by the reaction of the body's immune system to the injured one.[10] Modern drugs have virtually eliminated this phenomenon, but even in the early 1900s swift removal of the diseased eye would have prevented harm to the other one.

A renowned Washington eye specialist, Dr. Swann Burnett, finally removed the blinded left eye several weeks later and fitted Jamie with a glass replacement, but by then the damage was done. The eventual deterioration of Thurber's right eye and his ultimate blindness in the 1940s probably could have been avoided had he received prompt, proper treatment following the bow-and-arrow accident. Thurber always considered it a miracle that lacking, as he always insisted, "all apparatus for sight," he was able to see well enough with his troubled right eye to read, write, and draw for the next forty years. It wasn't true that his remaining eye lacked the equipment for vision, damaged though it was; but as his ophthalmologist and friend, Dr. Gordon Bruce, later observed, what Thurber lacked in the physical ability to see, he made up for with an acute visual imagination and raw determination.[11]

Although Thurber would demonstrate unusual fraternal generosity by supporting his brother William financially for decades, and never voiced any resentment over William's role in partially blinding him, he also never invited William to his various homes. He resented William's tendency to boast, years later, about his own perfect eyesight, and clearly found William's presence disquieting. And while Thurber relished his mother's eccentricities, mined them for story material, and was in all respects a faithful, devoted son, it is clear he also blamed her and his father for failing to get him timely treatment for the injury that would cause him such anguish and so profoundly alter his life.

The vagaries of politics brought an unexpected end to the Washington phase of Charles Thurber's career, and by early 1903 the family had returned to Columbus. There he got a job as a recording clerk in the Ohio Senate, but an attack of an otherwise undiagnosed "brain fever" in 1904 incapacitated him for months and forced the family to move into the mansion of Grandfather Fisher, who was a reluctant, sometimes abusive host. He took special delight in tormenting Jamie. In an effort to lessen the tensions, the family decided that Jamie ought to spend more time at the ramshackle home of the stocky, unconventional, widowed midwife who had delivered him, Margery Albright. Although no relation, "Aunt Margery" became a sort of second mother to Jamie, whose first piece of writing, at about age seven, was a poetic tribute entitled "My Aunt Margery Albright's Garden at 185 South Fifth Street, Columbus, Ohio." On occasion he would spend weeks on end there, charmed by the dilapidation of Aunt Margery's home and warmed by an affection absent in the Fisher manse.[12]

Because the loss of his left eye had forced him to miss a year of school in Washington, Jamie was a year behind when he entered Sullivant School, located in a working-class neighborhood, where many fellow students were a lot further behind in their studies than he was. Some of the fourth graders were teenagers. Fortunately for Jamie, he was befriended by a strapping black classmate named Floyd. "If Floyd was known to be on your side, nobody in the school would dare to be 'after' you and chase you home," Thurber recalled.[13]

His physical limitations prevented Jamie from participating in sports, much as he wanted to, so he became instead an enthusiastic spectator and enhanced his already superb memory for batting averages and other sporting statistics. His youthful delight in sports would never wane. He was a decent but often distracted student, capable of using a typewriter before he was seven but given to daydreaming. One object of his reveries was Eva Prout, a child star in vaudeville, for whom he retained an idealized devotion for years. One teacher at Sullivant thought Jamie was so inattentive that she told his mother he might be deaf.[14]

While Jamie was in the fourth grade at Sullivant, a teacher first took

7

notice of his interest in drawing and encouraged it. His parents were un-impressed. They thought the meticulous copies that his brother William made of Charles Dana Gibson's drawings were the original, inspired efforts of an artistic prodigy and told their second son (or so he re-called): "Don't bother William with your scrawls, Jamie; let him get his work done, he's going to be the artist."[15]

When Jamie moved on to the less-combative Douglas Junior High for seventh and eighth grades, he blossomed – to a degree. Remaining shy, quiet, tall, and gawky, he nevertheless began exhibiting a decided talent for writing that impressed his teachers and even won admira-tion from his classmates. He was given the honor of writing the "Class Prophecy" for the eighth graders of 1909, an essay whose traditional format dictated the mentioning of every class member's name in a tale set far in the future. Jamie's prophecy indirectly foreshadowed more about his future than anyone could have imagined. He wrote of how one classmate, Harold Young, builds a " 'Seairoplane' that travels in the water as well as thru the air and on the land." The class boards this wondrous machine for a trip across the United States and on to Mars. But then disaster strikes:

"Harold came rushing out of the engine room with dishevelled hair and bulging eyes. We asked him what on earth was the matter. For an answer he pointed to a piece of rope that was caught in a part of the farthest end of a long beam, which extended far over the side of the Seairoplane. Then he said, 'Unless that rope is gotten out of the curo-bater we will all be killed.' These awful words astounded us and we all became frightened at once. Suddenly amid all of our lamentations a cry from Harold was heard and we all looked up. What was our surprise to see James Thurber walking out on the beam. He reached the end safely and then extricated the rope, but when he turned to come back his foot caught and he pitched head foremost towards the deck. His unusual length saved him for he landed safely on the Seairoplane. We were all very joyful that the terrible crisis had been safely passed and afterwards learned that James was a tightrope walker with Barnsells and Ringbaileys circus." [16]

So it was that the classmates of half-blind, awkward, fourteen-year-old James Thurber got a preview peek into the secret life of Walter Mitty.

Entering East High School, Columbus's best, Jamie continued to shine, becoming, as he later put it, "just a woman teacher's pet," and something of a class leader. His first published story, a hokey Western saga entitled "The Third Bullet," appeared in *X-Rays*, the East High School magazine, which he longed to edit. Years later, he discovered that his mother had asked the school's principal to deny him the editorship because of his eye problems. Another ambition was not thwarted. He decided to run for senior class president in 1913 and won. He graduated with honors and gave the President's Address at the Class Day Program. It was a heady moment for an eighteen-year-old who had overcome major handicaps.[17]

The Thurber family finances did not allow for academic advancement to any private college in the Midwest or elsewhere. The rarefied Ivy League was out of the question. During the rambunctious 1912 presidential contest, which pitted incumbent Republican President (and Ohioan) William Howard Taft against his former patron, ex-President Theodore Roosevelt, running on the Progressive Bull Moose ticket, and Democrat Woodrow Wilson, Charles Thurber had quit his post with the State Republican Executive Committee and gone over to the Bull Moosers. This was an unusual exhibition of independence and idealism by the elder Thurber that his son James admired ever after, but like TR's third-party movement, it was a futile effort. Charles Thurber managed to hang on to a post with the much-diminished Progressive

Party until 1914, when work in one more unsuccessful gubernatorial campaign brought to a close that phase of his career.

By this time, the Thurber family had moved to 77 Jefferson Avenue, where they lived until 1917. This was the residence that Thurber later would immortalize in *My Life and Hard Times* as the boyhood home in which the bed fell on his father one night and where a ghost got in to frighten the Thurbers on another evening. He later said he deliberately changed the home's address in the book to a fictional 77 Lexington Avenue "for the simple reason that there *was* a ghost . . . [and] I didn't want to alarm whoever might be living there when I wrote the story." [18]

Although Thurber's academic goals and career objectives were vague, he had a restless, inquiring mind and knew he wanted to avoid his father's fate as a low-paid political drudge. Somewhere deep within him stirred ambitions never harbored by his brother Robert, weakened by a thyroid condition and interested primarily in collecting obscure books, and beyond the grasp of his brother William, a blustery pursuer of dubious business enterprises. Both remained in Columbus and ended up relying to a large extent on James's largess.

With just a week to spare, Thurber decided to enroll with the 1913 freshman class of the College of Arts, Philosophy, and Science at Ohio State University, a land-grant institution that was just what a financially strapped student needed: free. Ohio State, concerned mainly with agricultural education and engineering, had some distinguished faculty members at the time, such as Thurber's American history instructor, Arthur M. Schlesinger, Sr., and it produced some impressive students. It was not, however, an institution renowned for scholarship. Thurber later liked to sum up the reigning academic philosophy there by quoting the biting assessment of his favorite English professor, Joseph Villiers Denney: "Millions for manure but not one cent for literature."

The most distinctive aspects of campus life at Ohio State were activities denied to Thurber: <u>fraternities and football</u>. His physical limitations prevented participation in any athletics, and his personality and appearance failed to impress those arbiters of social acceptability, the members of various fraternities. By now six feet one and a half inches tall, painfully thin, poorly dressed, gangling and outwardly diffident, he was not asked to pledge any house and thus became an instant pariah.[19]

As disastrous as his debut at O.S.U. was, it at least provided experiences that became grand fodder, years later, for "University Days," one of the funniest chapters in *My Life and Hard Times*. Required by law to take military drill, he was an instinctively ineffectual soldier whose parade-ground gaffes prompted the school's blustery cadet corps commandant to bellow at him, "You are the main trouble with this university!" Gymnasium, also required, was no better. There Thurber was not allowed to wear his glasses and routinely "bumped into professors, horizontal bars, agricultural students, and swinging iron rings."[20]

During his singularly unpleasant freshman year, however, Thurber also obtained official academic confirmation of something he always knew he possessed: a phenomenal memory. In a general psychology class, a lengthy article was read aloud and the students were told to write everything they could remember from it. Thurber recalled an incredible 78 percent of the article's facts, and after a week had gone by he still could remember about half of them. His professor and classmates were astonished but Thurber was not. He was well aware of what he liked to term his "total recall," a skill he said he shared with his mother. Decades later, it would prove to be his salvation. After he went completely blind, Thurber was able to use his extraordinary memory to compose, rewrite and edit entire articles in his mind, preserving his career as well as his sanity.[21]

The pain of university life that freshman year far outweighed its pleasures for Thurber, so while he registered for the 1914–1915 academic year, he simply stopped going to most of his classes and did not get a single passing grade. He basically dropped out of school, told no one about it, and nobody seemed to notice – not his parents, his brothers, nor the school. Like many a teenager before and since, Thurber loved his parents but did not relate to them; in turn, they gave their moody, closed-mouthed second son a wide berth. He occasionally was seen on campus but more often simply vanished, perhaps hiding away in the library or going to the movies.

Eventually tiring of truancy, Thurber decided to try again and re-registered at Ohio State in the fall of 1915. In addition to his chronic problems with military drill and gym, he now encountered another impediment to academic advancement: botany class. He simply couldn't see through a microscope. "This used to enrage my instructor," Thurber wrote. The learned man wanted his students to study plant cells, but all Thurber could see was "what looked like a lot of milk," he told the instructor. "This, he claimed, was the result of my not having adjusted the microscope properly, so he would readjust it for me, or rather, for himself. And I would look again and see milk."

Thurber dropped out of botany class but had to sign up for it again the following year because a passing grade in one of the biological sciences was a requirement for graduation. The instructor vowed to make Thurber see plant cells by employing "every adjustment of the microscope known to man."

"With only one of them did I see anything but blackness or the familiar lacteal opacity, and that time I saw, to my pleasure and amazement, a variegated constellation of flecks, specks, and dots. These I hastily drew. The instructor, noting my activity, came back from an adjoining desk, a smile on his lips and his eyebrows high in hope. He looked at my cell drawing. 'What's that?' he demanded, with a hint of a squeal in his voice. 'That's what I saw,' I said. 'You didn't, you didn't, you *didn't!'* he screamed, losing control of his temper instantly, and he bent over and squinted into the microscope. His head snapped up. 'That's your eye!' he shouted. 'You've fixed the lens so that it reflects! You've drawn your eye!' " [22]

Thurber's repeated absences from military drill again threatened to end his college career, but O.S.U.'s indulgent, accommodating president, William Oxley Thompson, personally intervened on his behalf, enabling him to register again in the fall of 1916. "The great Thompson said to me, 'Don't let the military get you by the neck,' " Thurber recalled in a 1960 letter to a university contemporary. [23]

An equally important stroke of fortune that fall was Thurber's first encounter with fellow student Elliott Nugent, who would become the first of several influential mentors to spot the incipient genius within Thurber and encourage it to come out. The suave son of a prominent playwright and actor, J. C. Nugent, and himself a professional performer when not in school, the younger Nugent was impressed by the wit in one of Thurber's literature class compositions, began to cultivate his friendship, and even tried to alter his appearance, getting him a new suit of clothes and having his unruly thatch of hair trimmed. At Nugent's insistence, and probably with his financial assistance, Thurber was accepted into the Phi Kappa Psi social fraternity and joined the *Ohio State Lantern,* the student newspaper, the *Sundial,* the monthly literary and humor magazine, and the Strollers, the drama club. Almost miraculously, Thurber had become a man-about-campus, and he would always acknowledge Nugent's instrumental role in effecting the magical transformation. His accomplishments on campus were such that he was even elected to Sphinx, the honorary society for seniors. [24]

The first published examples of what Thurber characterized as "my so-called drawings" appeared in the *Sundial,* of which he became the editor-in-chief during the 1917–1918 academic year, and he was disinclined decades later to detect any improvement in his artistic efforts thereafter. His drawings, he wrote to a correspondent in 1950, "were very much the same then as they are now." He claimed to be far more embarrassed by his undergraduate writing and said he was "willing to pay enormous sums of money" for old copies of the *Sundial* in order to prevent exhumation of his literary juvenilia.[25]

The Nugent-inspired advancement of Thurber at O.S.U. was more than merely social and extracurricular. Suddenly Thurber also took an interest in his studies – and three special English professors took an interest in him. Joseph Villiers Denney, a Shakespearean scholar and dean of the College of Arts, was especially admired by Thurber as the witty, unflappable "imp of the faculty," and years later Denney served as the model for the wise and courageous Dean Damon in *The Male Animal,* the Broadway comedy Thurber wrote with Nugent about a fight over academic freedom at a Midwestern university very similar to Ohio State.[26]

As an intellectual and literary influence, Joseph Russell Taylor, exponent of Henry James, had a far greater impact on Thurber, who became a lifelong devotee of James and greatly admired, indeed often paraphrased, such Taylor maxims as "Nothing genuine need fear the test of laughter," and "Art is revision."[27]

Thurber found amusing as a curiosity, but did not admire, a third well-known English professor of the time, William Lucius Graves, commonly called Billy. He was an odd but popular teacher of short story writing whose preferences for the mawkish magazine tales of the period served as an unintentionally instructive counterpoint to the artistic principles advocated by Taylor. Thurber was unimpressed by Graves and chose to take a "deferred pass" in his course, having declined to write the stories Graves directed his students to compose to prefabricated plots.[28]

In addition to the examples they set for Thurber either to emulate or avoid, all three professors apparently were keen observers of the potential talent he possessed. Nelson Budd, a contemporary of Thurber's at O.S.U., claimed that Denney, Taylor, and Graves all told him at one time or another that Thurber was destined for literary greatness.[29]

He was not, however, destined to get a degree.

Most of his friends already were in the armed forces following U.S. entry into World War I, but his own military participation was debarred by his partial blindness. Since his academic record still was thirty-three credits short of the number required for graduation, and the seemingly insurmountable gymnasium, science, and drill requirements had yet to be met, Thurber found himself a twenty-three-year-old junior after five years in college with scant prospects for successfully completing his senior year. So he dropped out of school in the spring of 1918 and thus became the sort of distinguished alumnus fit for a Thurberish tale: the renowned student, lionized in later years, who never graduated.

Although he was relieved to have been rejected for combat because of his glass eye, Thurber was not unpatriotic. He wished to find something he could do in the war — and out of town. Living at home had become oppressive. His father, a minor bureaucrat without peer, heard about a U.S. State Department program for training code clerks in Washington, with overseas postings likely for the best trainees. Ohio State's President Thompson again assisted by providing a letter of recommendation, Thurber's father pulled the few small strings available to him, and Thurber went off to Washington, where he landed a spot in a cryptography class along with several dozen other would-be decoders, including the future poet Stephen Vincent Benét. Benét would later remember Thurber as an exceptionally skillful cryptographer, "an expert at solving difficult and improbable messages."[30]

In Washington, Thurber studied hard, hung out in local newspaper haunts – a preference established when he was an editor of the O.S.U. student paper – and wrote long, often embarrassingly juvenile letters to his former mentor, Nugent, addressing them "Dear old Pythias," "My dear old confrere Nugey," or "Dear Bringer of Wisteria into Waste Places," and signing them "Jim in old Phi Psi forever." He wrote of potential romances that never ripened, of the influenza epidemic, of a fantasy novel he was planning that contained foreshadowings of the delightful fairy tales he would compose years later.[31]

Thurber's training as a code clerk lasted more than three months – and practically outlasted the war. He was posted to Paris but did not sail for France until ten days before the armistice. He docked there, depleted by seasickness, on November 13, 1918, two days after the guns went silent. His war was over but his life beyond Ohio had at last begun.

2

Columbus Days and Paris Nights

Thurber's mother had larded his luggage with Hershey bars, correctly anticipating food shortages and high prices in war-depleted Paris, but his suitcases were shipped separately and lost. They didn't arrive until five months later — by which time the candy bars had melted all over his clothes.

In the interim, he had gone to a store billing itself as "Jack, American Tailor," bought an ill-fitting suit that "might have been made by the American Can Company," and trudged to various hat shops in a vain search for some sort of headgear that didn't make him look ridiculous.[1] He also reported to the American Peace delegation's headquarters at the Hotel Crillon and the office of Colonel Edward M. House, the personal representative of President Woodrow Wilson. House supposedly had requested the assistance of twelve or fifteen code clerks, but in fact what he apparently had sought were twelve or fifteen copies of the American code book. The request somehow had been botched in transatlantic transmission and a phalanx of young decipherers had been dispatched instead.

The colonel's frustrated staff sent Thurber and his colleagues to the American Embassy, where they toiled in a tedium that was, in Thurber's case, relieved by the excitement of touring a Paris finally free of war, and visiting the still shell-pocked and booby-trapped battlefields nearby. In Reims he stumbled over one such trap and set it off, later saying in a letter home that while there "wasn't much of an explosion – a sharp report like a pistol – and no pieces of the stuff fell very near . . . , I'm admitting herewith quite frankly that I was scared badly."[2]

He also found, while wandering Paris and the countryside, that he was torn between the allures of libertine France and the strictures of his Victorian upbringing in Columbus, for which he remained home-sick. "My heart is in Ohio," he wrote to his brother Robert, but his virginity was left behind in Paris. Shortly before he turned twenty-five, he encountered a show girl from the Folies-Bergère with whom he took what he later called his "first step aside."[3]

This major accomplishment notwithstanding, Thurber was frus-trated by – and envious of – the professional achievements of Elliott Nugent, now a graduate of Ohio State and embarked full-time on a playwriting and acting career. So after sixteen months abroad, Thurber decided early in 1920 to return to Columbus, although he had no precise idea of what he would do when he got home. As he wrote to Nugent, however, he was certain that embarking "on the old road of life . . . in my case can mean but one thing, writing."[4]

With a rented typewriter, he began by devising opuses for The Stroll-ers, his old college theater group, and for a local, all-male theatrical troupe, the Scarlet Mask Club. His only income-producing employ-ment, however, was a clerical position with the Ohio Department of Agriculture, surely a dispiriting spot for a young man who had, after all, seen Paris. Even worse was his source of extra pocket money, a job in the ticket booth of the side shows at the Ohio State Fair. Finally, he was hired as a cub reporter for the *Columbus Dispatch* at twenty-five dollars a week and came under the fearsome tutelage of the city editor, Norman "Gus" Kuehner, who taunted him with the nickname "Phi Beta Kappa," scorning not Thurber's failure to graduate from college but the fact he had gone there at all. When Thurber scooped the paper's police reporter by getting the high school yearbook photo of a drowned boy, Kuehner rewarded his enterprise by making him City Hall reporter – and changing his nickname to "Author." He knew Thurber had literary ambitions beyond the City Hall beat.[5]

The first City Council meeting Thurber attended was interrupted by a fire that burned down the City Hall. He got a five-dollar raise for his crisp account of it, which was the centerpiece of an extra edition of the *Dispatch*. He soon became, he boasted thirty years later, "the tough Gus Kuehner's top boy." He was given some choice assignments, such as the dedication of Ohio Stadium, allowed to write occasional theater and movie reviews, and even was sent to New York to review plays and write profiles of such celebrities as Al Jolson. Also among those he wrote about were Elliott Nugent and his father, both doing well on Broadway. During this trip, Thurber served as best man at Nugent's wedding, which took place just before the matinee performance of *Dulcy,* the play in which Nugent was appearing.[6]

Back in Columbus, Thurber encountered an erstwhile New York newspaperman, John McNulty, doing time on the *Ohio State Journal* after having argued and imbibed his way out of journalistic jobs in Manhattan. McNulty's wit, writing skill, and way with a practical joke made him a boon companion for Thurber, who years later would see to it that readers of *The New Yorker* got to know McNulty, too.

Thurber's professional advancement, modest though it was and largely confined to Columbus, was more than matched in the spring of 1922 by a private development that astonished his family and friends: He contrived to meet and quickly marry Althea Adams, a comely twenty-one-year-old coed at Ohio State whose photo he had seen in an O.S.U. yearbook and had promptly determined to wed. Close friends were baffled by his swift conquest of the stunning, sophisticated, some-what imperious Althea; they couldn't figure out how he managed it.

Thurber's family thought the roles had been reversed: Althea, aggressive and ambitious, had set her cap for Jamie. They didn't like her – and the antipathy was heartily reciprocated. In particular, an instant animosity developed between Althea and Thurber's mother. To those who knew them both, the personalities of the manic, offbeat Mame Thurber and waspish, domineering Althea seemed destined to clash. In fact their traits were later combined in the Thurber Woman of story and cartoon. It was an analysis Thurber readily acknowledged and accepted. In later years, when he attributed his sense of humor to his mother, he also admitted that the light yet pointed stories he wrote in 1928 and 1929 about the domestic travails and tensions of young Mr. and Mrs. John Monroe were "transcripts" taken directly from his uneasy first marriage. He would later say of Althea, "She always scared me." * [7]

Thurber supplemented his income from the *Dispatch* by writing free-lance articles for the *Christian Science Monitor,* which paid him a princely eight to ten dollars a column but repeatedly botched his byline, identifying him as "Miss Jane Thurber." He was also a stringer for the *Cleveland News Leader,* and acted as a press agent for a concert manager who booked appearances in the hinterlands for such renowned performers as Sergei Rachmaninoff and others. Thurber continued writing theatrical pieces for The Strollers and the Scarlet Mask Club, for which Althea became a costume designer and assistant on lighting and scenery. With Scarlet Mask, he earned about $350 per play, directed and

---

*Thurber's daughter from that marriage, Rosemary, says it was fear, in fact, that her mother masked with brusqueness. "My mother's father died when she was seven or eight, and . . . she said her mother just didn't understand what to do with this big, hulking girl, so I think my mother was just very insecure. And she always seemed angry to me. But what I discovered in my maturity was that she was scared. And it came out in this kind of toughness." [8]

20

toured with the company, and even acted with it on occasion, which he loved. But Althea largely took charge of Thurber's life – and finances. She allotted him lunch money and carfare when he went off to work, and began urging him to look beyond Columbus for employment.[9]

Thurber was ready for a change. He was stagnating at the *Dispatch,* despite an opportunity he was given by the Sunday paper in 1923 to fill half a page with whatever he wished to write. The result was "Credos and Curios," a column in which he experimented with various essay forms, voiced often-contradictory views on literature and the strengths and weaknesses of his city and state, and emulated or praised the newspaper writers he admired most: H. L. Mencken, Finley Peter Dunne, Franklin P. Adams, and Columbus's own Robert O. Ryder, crafter of concise, witty observations. Like Adams's then-celebrated *New York World* column, "The Conning Tower," Thurber's effort combined verse and prose, froth with substance, commentary on public issues with ruminations on private concerns. Years later, Thurber accurately assessed the forty-two half-pages he wrote that year as "practice and spadework by a man of 28 who sometimes sounds 19." [10]

Nevertheless, "Credos and Curios" contained forerunners of some of Thurber's most famous pieces – and nearly forty years later he even resurrected the column's title for the anthology of his work he was planning just prior to his death. Like many a writer before and since, Thurber saved everything, revised constantly, and recycled whenever he could. In those *Dispatch* columns, he spoofed analytical studies of sex, described the peculiarities of his family, wrote short articles that featured reminiscences and word games, recounted personal mishaps, and parodied popular fiction and verse.

Whatever the failings of Thurber's "Credos and Curios" pieces, the feature was canceled through no fault of his own. Something printed on the other half of that Sunday feature page ruffled the sensibilities of some Pooh-Bahs in Urbana, Ohio. Their displeasure was sufficient to persuade the *Dispatch*'s worried publisher to kill the whole page.

Thurber also was infuriated and discouraged by the emasculation of a feature story he had written about a huge open-air meeting of the Ku Klux Klan — an event the more courageous *Ohio State Journal,* edited by his idol Robert O. Ryder, had covered in full. Bitter about being so unfairly deprived of his small measure of celebrity, as well as the opportunity to grow as a writer, he was increasingly responsive to Althea's insistence that they move to New York. As was the case several times in Thurber's life, he needed someone else to encourage, motivate, and push him ahead; his second wife, Helen, later likened her determined predecessor to a martinet in drag who shrewdly saw Thurber as her ticket out of Columbus and provided the impetus he needed to make the break.[11]

It was not at first as clean a break as Thurber, or Althea, may have wished. The *Dispatch* had a standing policy aimed at stifling any itch its reporters had to go elsewhere: those who quit were never rehired. Thurber was apprehensive about abandoning steady employment, but Althea finally persuaded him to accept an acquaintance's offer of a cabin in Jay, New York, a small town in the Adirondacks, as a writing retreat during the summer of 1924. With a little money saved and a few free-lance opportunities available, they decided to take the chance. Thurber quit the paper and they moved to the remote cottage, where Thurber diligently labored on a musical comedy libretto that later was lost on the subway, and on comic essays and short stories, most of which earned only rejection notices from the major magazines. Only one piece produced during this period — "Josephine Has Her Day" — finally was printed in the *Kansas City Star*'s Sunday magazine early in 1926.

"Josephine" was the tale of the purchase of a sickly puppy by a young

husband and wife who then give it away, try to reclaim it, and ultimately get it back from the dog's brutish new owner after a bizarre
battle in a rural grocery store. It was the first short story Thurber ever
managed to sell, and thirty years later he reprinted it in an anthology,
Thurber's Dogs, drolly noting that he had thought of "tinkering" with
its "noisy, uninevitable and improbable climax," but decided that doing
so would be "a kind of tampering with literary evidence," embarrass-
ing though that evidence may be. He also came to the conclusion that
the awkward ending demonstrated that he "apparently always had a
suppressed desire to take part in a brawl in a grocery." [12]

Broke after a summer of fruitless free-lancing, Thurber and Althea
were forced to return to Columbus, where the *Dispatch,* as it had promised, refused to rehire him. Thurber nevertheless rebounded, keeping
busy with a new production for the Scarlet Mask Club and promotional
work as a press agent for the Cleveland Symphony Orchestra – as well
as a circus, an amusement park, a movie theater, and other clients.

Remarkably, by early 1925, Thurber was earning more money as a
press agent than he had as a reporter. Even though he still was unsuccessfully trying to sell short stories, he might have been content to
stay in Columbus. Althea was not. She was convinced that Thurber was
destined for greater things and more exciting places than central Ohio.
She set her sights on France, where expatriate writers and artists by
the shipload were congregating. Once again, she persuaded Thurber to
leave his hometown. He later observed: "It is the women who love the
insecurity before they are thirty. Althea forced me to give up my good
paying jobs in Columbus and sail for France." [13]

They set sail in May 1925 and settled in a dismal farmhouse in Normandy. Thurber at first attempted to write a novel but soon abandoned
it and the countryside for Paris and reporting. Many other impover-
ished American writers also were looking for work on the city's two

English-language newspapers – the Paris editions of the *New York Herald* and the *Chicago Tribune* – but Thurber had a significant advantage over most of them: he actually had been a reporter. Although the more prominent *Herald* spurned him, the city editor of the scruffier *Tribune* hired him on the spot when he heard that Thurber could write headlines and had spent time on a newspaper. He was set to work on the night copy desk, at twelve dollars a week, rewriting items clipped from French newspapers, trying to write complete stories out of cryptic cable reports from the United States, and sometimes manufacturing outlandish quotes and tales for the amusement of himself and "the other slaves." [14]

Soon joining Thurber on the copy desk was a thin, twenty-one-year-old pipe-smoker named William L. Shirer, who found the "lanky, owl-eyed man with thick glasses" to be a warm, friendly colleague, a "genius" at fleshing out the meager cable reports, and an incorrigible prankster. Given a spare eight or ten words from the cable and told to write an entire column based on them, Thurber would purse his lips, say "Yes, suh," and cheerfully confect accounts that perhaps conveyed the essence of an event more than what actually occurred. [15] He was especially good at inventing authentic-sounding inanities to attribute to President Calvin Coolidge, then at the height of his powers as an enunciator of the obvious. Usually Thurber came up with these bogus quotes to pad a story about a speech the president actually had given, but sometimes the speech itself was a Thurberish invention. Once, when asked to provide a brief item to fill an empty spot on a page, Thurber blithely tapped out a Washington dateline and wrote: " 'A man who does not pray is not a praying man,' President Coolidge today told the annual convention of the Protestant Church of America." It fitted neatly into the spot and was dutifully published. [16]

On another occasion, a piece of Thurber's fictionalized news nearly made it into the paper and almost got him canned. He composed a juicy story of international intrigue featuring robbery, rape, blackmail, adultery, gambling, and gun-running that involved ten to twenty internationally known celebrities and statesmen. Set in type by a French compositor who didn't understand English, it was all ready to run under a blazing headline when it caught the eye of the *Tribune*'s managing editor, David Darrah, who quickly pulled it. Years later, Thurber wrote to a friend that while Darrah had been enraged over the story, saying it would have cost the *Tribune* "eight million dollars' worth of libel," the editor had lectured him "only mildly" about it. Shirer, in his memoirs, recalled Darrah "almost fired the apologetic Thurber on the spot." [17]

Other reporters whose fabricated stories did get into the paper were not so lucky. One writer, Spencer Bull, decided to enliven a mundane press release about a visit to Paris by the then-Prince of Wales, later briefly Edward VIII and subsequently Duke of Windsor. The official release described the prince's review of a group of British Boy Scouts. Bull wickedly added a few sentences on how the prince, upon asking a youngster his name, was told by the youth, "None of your goddamned business, sir." In response, "the Prince snatched a riding crop from his equerry and beat the boy's brains out," Bull wrote. The story was printed and Bull was fired.[18]

Work at the Paris *Tribune* was not all wacadoo pranks. Its small staff tried to put out a reputable paper as well as they could with sparse resources – no library of background clips, a telegram of a few hundred words a day from the home paper's London bureau, a daily cable of just 100 words from the New York office. One night in the fall of 1925, Thurber's incredible memory and creativity were put to far better use than concocting Coolidge quotes when the *Tribune*'s city editor handed him a five-word cable dispatch that read: "Christy Mathewson died tonight Saranac." It was all Thurber needed. A walking encyclopedia of baseball anecdotes and statistics, he simply sat down and produced what Shirer remembered as "one of the finest tributes I have ever read, replete with facts about the player's pitching records, stories of some of the great games he had pitched in World Series, and an assessment of his character on and off the diamond." As he would demonstrate many times in the years to come, when called upon to write a warm tribute to a departed relative, friend, idol, or even a pet, no one was better at it than Thurber.[19]

On another memorable night, Shirer recalled, an intoxicated F. Scott Fitzgerald stumbled into the *Tribune*'s city room, plopped down at the copy desk, and demanded that the staff join him in song while he tried to grab copies of the stories they were working on and tear them up. As disruptive as Fitzgerald was in the city room, he turned out to be even more obstreperous when Thurber, Shirer, and two other *Tribune* men tried to take him home. Maneuvering him into a taxi after a whirlwind tour of some bars, the newspapermen finally got Fitzgerald to the front of his apartment house, where his wife, Zelda, appeared at an open window to yell at him and he balked at going in. Breaking away from his escorts, he ran around the would-be samaritans, grabbed a piece of iron grating from the base of a curbside tree, and nearly bludgeoned Thurber with it, going at him on his blind side before one of the other reporters succeeded in wrestling the author of *The Great Gatsby* to the ground. The newsmen then managed to carry Fitzgerald into the apartment house and graciously decline the offer of another drink from the suddenly hospitable Zelda.* [20]

---

*In his own recollection of Fitzgerald, "Scott in Thorns," published in 1951, Thurber chose to forget this entire incident and said that a long, bibulous, and friendly evening he spent with Fitzgerald following a chance meeting in a New York bar in 1934 was the only encounter he had with him.[21]

Thurber and Althea spent the winter of 1925–1926 in Nice, where the proprietors of the *Tribune* had decided to send seven or eight staffers to put out a six-page Riviera edition of the paper. Althea was appointed society editor, which gave the Thurbers some essential extra income. What Thurber later called these "long days of warm blue weather" were perhaps the happiest of his often-troubled first marriage, and he relished the memories of them for the rest of his life. When a scholar of American humor wrote in 1942 that Thurber had endured "drudgery on several newspapers," Thurber's mocking demurrer, "Memoirs of a Drudge," contained a glowing reminiscence of this time of "pure joy." Since he and his fellow scribes got the bulk of their copy by wire from Paris, they had only to write headlines for the most part, "a pleasurable occupation if you are not rushed, and we were never rushed." Inventing news fillers, an amusing sideline in Paris, became a major sport in the south of France.

We went to work after dinner and usually had the last chronicle of the diverting day written and ready for the linotypers well before midnight. It was then our custom to sit around for half an hour, making up items for the society editor's column. She was too pretty, we thought, to waste the soft southern days tracking down the arrival of prominent persons on the Azure Coast. So all she had to do was stop in at the Ruhl and the Negresco each day and pick up the list of guests who had just registered. The rest of us invented just enough items to fill up the last half of her column, and a gay and romantic cavalcade, indeed, infested the littoral of our imagination. "Lieutenant General and Mrs. Pendelton Gray Winslow," we would write, "have arrived at their villa, Heart's Desire, on Cap d'Antibes, bringing with them their prize Burmese monkey, Thibalt". . . . In this manner we turned out, in no time at all, and with the expenditure of very little mental energy, the most glittering column of social notes in the history of the American newspaper, either here or abroad.

As the hour of midnight struck . . . , the late Frank Harris would often drop in at the *Tribune* office, and we would listen to stories of Oscar Wilde, Walt Whitman, Bernard Shaw, Emma Goldman, and Frank Harris. Thus ran the harsh and exacting tenor of those days of slavery.[22]

There were brief encounters with other exotic individuals then on the Côte d'Azur: Thurber had to give Isadora Duncan the news about the suicide of her former husband, Serge Yessenin; he interviewed the shifty-eyed financier Harry Sinclair, a key figure in the Teapot Dome scandal, and movie idol Rudolph Valentino; he covered the epic tennis match in Cannes between Helen Wills and Suzanne Lenglen.[23]

He experienced some success as a free-lancer, selling travel and feature articles to American newspapers and magazines. Readers of the *New York World* saw his interview with the Frenchman who had been Woodrow Wilson's barber during the Versailles Peace Conference and still considered him the world's savior; the *New York Herald*'s readers learned about historian Arthur Bigelow Paine's pursuit of Joan of Arc's white armor; residents of Kansas City who bought the *Star* were advised that French cabbies and bellhops always had their hands out ("'Tip, Tip, Hurray!' The Battle Cry of Greedom"); the subscribers to slick, sophisticated *Harper's* were treated to an amusing analysis of the differences between French and American sidewalk fisticuffs in "A Sock in the Jaw – French Style." *Harper's* paid Thurber a staggering ninety dollars for this piece, he enjoyed recalling, and he never again felt as rich as he did when that check arrived.[24]

Such professional achievements and supplemental income were infrequent, however, and both his finances and his marriage remained shaky. It was costly to live on the Riviera, and Althea had become interested in one of his newspaper colleagues. Thurber realized that the Riviera, and even Paris, were turning out to be a professional dead end, charming though they were. He brooded in what Shirer recalled as "a black mood of despair," fearing he was doomed to hackdom or failure. He didn't know what his literary future held, and the example set by Fitzgerald and Ernest Hemingway, then both in Paris and younger than he, was not encouraging. He said to Shirer, "A guy has to face it. I'm thirty-one going on thirty-two and I ain't going to be no novelist. . . . I ain't going to be no Fitzgerald or Hemingway. Look what they've done, and they're not yet thirty." [25]

Whatever success he might attain, Thurber decided, would be back in the States, in New York, not overseas. He had to borrow the money to return home while his wife chose to remain in France for the time being. He was glum as he sailed for New York. In a shipboard letter to an old friend in Columbus, he offered a gloomy assessment of his abilities: "I write mostly soi-disant humor since I haven't brains enough to write more solid articles and wouldn't if I could. I often worry about my future since I am no doctor and at best a mean scrivener, but out of all the things one does, from pipe fitting to testing seamless leather belting and from ceramics to statesmanship, I can do only one thing, even passably, and that is to make words and space them between punctuation points." [26]

He landed in New York in June 1926, a thirty-one-year-old erstwhile expatriate with a temporarily dim view of his own talents and only ten dollars in his pocket. His prospects did not seem pleasing.

3

The Seal Barks

With an ignominious return to Columbus and press agentry an unappealing alternative, Thurber found a five-dollar-a-week room in Greenwich Village and set to work trying to recycle old articles and write new ones.[1]

He showed the resulting products of his industry to a literary agent, who suggested that he submit them to *The New Yorker,* a slim, even skimpy new humor magazine, which had earned a smidgen of notoriety. Thurber sent the pieces to *The New Yorker,* and all of them were turned down by a now-forgotten editor, John Chapin Mosher, a virtual "rejection machine" who, Thurber recalled years later, looked "like a professor of English literature who has not approved of the writing of anybody since Sir Thomas Browne." Bludgeoned but undaunted, Thurber began working on a mammoth spoof of current bestsellers, including George Dorsey's *Why We Behave Like Human Beings* and Paul de Kruif's *Microbe Hunters.* He called his epic *Why We Behave Like Microbe Hunters.* It violated one of the key requirements of parody — brevity — by running to some 30,000 words, and it, too, was promptly rejected by magazines and book publishers.[2]

Althea at last returned from France later that summer, and Thurber was on the verge of going back to Ohio when almost simultaneously he was offered a reporter's job on the *Evening Post* and Franklin P. Adams devoted one of his "Conning Tower" columns to a parody of Thurber's that *The New Yorker* had rejected: "If Tabloids Had Covered the Famous Sport 'Love-Death' Scandal of Hero and Leander." ("LOVE PACT BARED / AS LEANDER DROWNS! – Daily Tab. Sept. 15, SWIMMER MISSING IN / HELLESPONT CROSSING – Daily Glass, Sept. 15," and so on.)[3]

It proved to be an important morale booster, which is not an inconsequential item to a struggling writer.

At the *Evening Post,* Thurber first was assigned to cover general news, an area in which he achieved more renown for ineptitude than enterprise. On being dispatched to Brooklyn to cover a huge fire, he got so lost on the subway that he abandoned it for a cab, only to pass a newsstand carrying copies of the *Post* bearing banner headlines about the blaze – over stories obtained from other sources. "A four-alarm fire," his editor later fumed, "and this fellow can't find it!"[4]

On another occasion, the editors decreed that the leads to all news stories be as brief as possible. Thurber's means of compliance:

"Dead.

"That was what the man was the police found in an areaway last night."[5]

In due course, the *Post*'s editors realized where Thurber's true talents were and shifted him from hard news to features, where he found that unlike the doors often faced by regular reporters, "the portals of the fantastic and the unique are always left open" to the feature writer. He "studied gypsies in Canarsie and generals in the Waldorf, listened to a man talk backwards and watched a blindfolded boy play ping-pong."[6] He also scored a few scoops, wangling an exclusive interview with the usually unapproachable inventor of the lightbulb and phonograph, Thomas Alva Edison (who kept insisting that the upstart medium of radio "will always distort the soprano voice"), and persuading the widow of Harry Houdini to discuss the magician's extensive

collection of books on crime, penology, psychic phenomena, and presti-
digitation. Mrs. Houdini even gave Thurber seventy-five books from
her husband's library, further fueling an interest he had in Houdini that
lasted the rest of his life.[7]

The approbation he earned from such stories, as well as the five-
dollar bonuses he got for his scoops, were some satisfaction; but what
he – and Althea – really wanted was success with *The New Yorker*
or some other publication that offered him a more promising future
than the *Evening Post*. Instead, he still had only rejection slips. Althea
decided that he was laboring too long over his free-lance articles and
suggested that he allow himself only forty-five minutes to compose a
piece. Thurber set an alarm clock to fit the deadline and began writing.
Parodying such popular crazes of the day as flagpole-sitting, he quickly
drafted a tale about a small, unassuming man who sets a world's record
for going around inside the revolving door of a department store. *The
New Yorker* snapped it up. Called "An American Romance," the piece
prefigures Thurber's skill at using satire to critique American values. A
foolish exercise is rewarded extravagantly and the hero's only remark
is the bathetic "I did it for the wife and children."[8]

Having finally breached the barricades at *The New Yorker,* Thurber
soon thereafter met Elwyn Brooks White, known to his friends as
Andy, a staff writer on the magazine who would become, as had Elliott
Nugent, a mentor whose influence was crucial to Thurber's emergence
from obscurity. Just as Nugent's encouragement and support brought
Thurber out of the shadows at Ohio State, so E. B. White's literary example, and selfless promotion of Thurber as a writer and cartoonist,
shaped and nurtured the extraordinary comic talent bubbling beneath
the surface of Thurber's often distracted and brooding exterior. And
just as Thurber always acknowledged Nugent's assistance when he was
in college, he forever credited White as the one who really taught him

how to write. "Until I learned discipline in writing from studying Andy White's stuff, I was a careless, nervous, headlong writer," Thurber wrote to a friend in 1956, nearly thirty years after he met White. "The precision and clarity of White's writing helped me a lot, slowed me down from the dogtrot of newspaper tempo and made me realize that a writer turns on his mind, not a faucet."[9]

Thurber's recollection of his February 1927 meeting with White varied as to details; what was certain is that White and he got along well from the start. White thought Thurber might fit in on the then-tiny staff of *The New Yorker,* and promptly arranged to introduce him to the redoubtable Harold W. Ross, founding editor of the magazine, who hired Thurber immediately.

Ross, an amalgam of contradictions, was surely one of the most brilliant and bizarre figures in American journalism. He alternately intrigued, delighted, and infuriated almost everyone who dealt with him, and none more so than Thurber. A fanatic about the facts, details, grammar, and punctuation in his magazine's stories, Ross was so disinterested in his own finances that his private secretary was able to steal $71,000 from his bank account without arousing any suspicion.[10] A gangling, ill-educated son of Colorado who was raised in Washington State and worked on newspapers in Utah, California, and other far-flung venues, he became a caliph of Manhattan who edited a magazine that was the epitome of sophistication – yet some of its sophisticated (and not-so-sophisticated) humor had to be explained to him. He was a man of refined literary sensibility who was ignorant of many literary classics. He reveled in reminiscences of his newspaper days yet sought to purge conventional journalism from his magazine.

Ross fascinated and perplexed Thurber, who spent years trying to capture and illuminate in prose the inexplicable nature of Ross's genius. *The Years with Ross,* Thurber's popular and entertaining 1959 memoir *cum* biography of *The New Yorker*'s founder, was also his most controversial book, and it ultimately cost him the friendship of White. In it, Thurber praised Ross as "the most remarkable man I have ever known and the greatest editor,"[11] but also portrayed him as a man whose eccentricities bordered on buffoonery. It was a characterization and portrayal with which White – and many other *New Yorker* veterans – took vehement exception.

If Thurber was unable to understand Ross, the editor initially misjudged Thurber, mistakenly envisaging him as an editor, not a writer. "Writers are a dime a dozen, Thurber," Ross told him. "What I want is an editor." Indeed, what Ross was seeking, Thurber recalled, was a supereditor, a "miracle man" or "Jesus," who would somehow transform the spontaneous but often harried and haphazard process by which the magazine was produced into a model of efficiency. He wanted someone to "make this place operate like a business office," and the improbable person Ross chose for this assignment, as Thurber recalled it, was himself.

In *The Years with Ross*, Thurber said he was made managing editor of the magazine in March 1927, worked seven days a week, often late into the night, wrote articles for which he was not paid extra, had to confer with other editors on "technical matters," and was called upon to sign the payroll each week. After a few months of this ordeal, Thurber wrote, he was "losing my weight, my grip and possibly my mind."[12]

Frustrated though he may have been at *The New Yorker* in 1927, what Thurber was not during this period was managing editor of the magazine. That post was held between 1925 and 1930 by Ralph Ingersoll, "the very administrative expert Ross was looking for," as Thurber paradoxically acknowledged, and by no one else thereafter. Thurber even claimed to have bawled out Ross for losing Ingersoll when the latter left to work for Henry Luce. What Thurber had been hired to be

Home

"He's having all his books translated into French.
They lose something in the original."

Thurber and his circle

"Have you seen my pistol, Honey-bun?"

was the magazine's "Sunday editor," with responsibility for editing the sports department, and as a writer on the side. Those who were irked by Thurber's recollections of Ross were as annoyed by his exaggeration of his original role at *The New Yorker* as by his dwelling on Ross's fallibilities.[13]

Regardless of his title and responsibilities at *The New Yorker,* by the summer of 1927 Thurber needed a vacation. Ross gave him two weeks off and he headed for Columbus with Althea and a Scottish terrier named Jeannie that they had purchased with the money he got from *The New Yorker* for his man-in-the-revolving-door story. When they were preparing to head back east, Jeannie disappeared and they spent two extra days hunting for her. Upon Thurber's return to the office, an outraged Ross berated him for extending his vacation to look for a lost dog, adding, "I consider that the act of a sis." Thurber, possessed of a hair-trigger temper, as he put it, exploded at this denigration of his masculinity. He demanded that Ross, who abhorred violence, get up and fight like a man – and get a friend to help him. "Who do you suggest?" Ross asked. "Alexander Woollcott!" Thurber yelled, naming the flabby and slightly effeminate theater critic who had been an Army buddy of Ross's in France. Ross began to laugh, "a wonderful, room-filling laugh" that "cooled the air like summer rain," Thurber recalled. They went out for a drink together at Tony's, a famous speakeasy, and began what Thurber remembered as "a lasting and deepening friendship." Soon after that brief blowup, Ross granted Thurber his wish and "demoted" him from editor to full-time writer.[14]

The writing staff that Thurber joined at *The New Yorker* was one of the most celebrated ever assembled. Ross had a superb instinct for recognizing talent, and in addition to White his regular staff members and contributors already included Wolcott Gibbs, Dorothy Parker, Alexander Woollcott, Russel Crouse, and Robert Benchley, whose brilliantly understated comic essays, parodies, and deft nonsense pieces had a profound influence on Thurber. The great terror of any humorist, Thurber later wrote, was the fear that something over which he had just sweated blood had been done faster and better by Benchley years before.* [15]

Thurber shared many traits with Benchley. Both were baffled by anything mechanical; both were inept with automobiles (Benchley refused to drive, and Thurber, in part because of his poor eyesight, was apprehensive behind the wheel); both were adept at acting and enjoyed performing; both drank more than was good for them – although Benchley remained convivial when drunk and Thurber became combative. Both were wonderfully funny as woebegone chroniclers of their own inadequacies.

Since the days of Benjamin Franklin's Poor Richard, the paragon of American wit had been the wise fool, the unlettered bumpkin who outsmarted the city slicker. The last example of that tradition was Will Rogers. Just as Rogers was at the apex of his career in the 1920s and early 1930s, another collection of humorists gained prominence, a group aptly described by critic Bernard DeVoto as the "Perfect Neurotics." They portrayed themselves as clumsy, insecure, inhibited and

---

*In "The Incomparable Mr. Benchley," an affectionate memorial essay, Thurber readily acknowledged that a 1935 Benchley story about a "day dreamer, cool and witty on the witness stand," and a 1932 Benchley piece dealing with fantasies of heroic peril "antedated a little old day dreamer of my own named Mitty." Benchley remains a model – and potential nemesis – for humorists today. Art Buchwald has said he stopped reading Benchley "because he had thought of every good idea before I did . . . [and] he inhibited me." Erma Bombeck says, "Bob Benchley is bone china to my Melmac," and Russell Baker says he sometimes browses through his Benchley books to "see if there is anything I can steal." [16]

frustrated, prone to daydreams in an effort to escape the harsh, unsympathetic world and petty annoyances that bedevil us all.[17] What Benchley called the "impedimenta of our daily life" and Thurber characterized as the "little perils of routine living" were often their favorite subject, with Thurber's ruminations upon them having a frequently darker undertone. The best humor, he believed, "is closest to . . . that part of the familiar which is distressing, even tragic," and those who write such humor live "an existence of jumpiness and apprehension." They "have a genius for getting into minor difficulties" and talk "largely about small matters and smally about great affairs."[18]

Although he may have shared a sense of ineptitude and subject matter with Benchley, Thurber shared a small office with E. B. White. It was a room "just big enough for two men and two typewriters," as White recalled. It also had lots of copy paper on which Thurber doodled even more than he wrote, a propensity and skill that White keenly recognized was worthy of encouragement.[19]

White excelled at writing "casuals," a type of brief essay conceived by Ross but given life by White. Ross wanted every casual, whether fiction, spoof, parody, nonsense, or anecdotal story or commentary, to be conversational, offhand, apparently effortless, like banter over cocktails or dinner. It is an exceedingly difficult form to master, and Thurber could closely observe White at work on it daily and read the results. White, in turn, enjoyed Thurber's work and, more by example than instruction, influenced its development and direction. Between them they wrote almost all of the "Talk of the Town" section of the magazine from 1927 to 1936. The "Notes and Comment" essays were written by White, while Thurber produced original reports and rewrote many of the stories submitted by other "Talk" staffers. Thurber became a master of easygoing style, blending crisp reportage with the elements of an erudite yet comic essay. In large measure, he and White created the tone of sophisticated, understated wit that established *The New Yorker*'s reputation.[20]

Thurber's own reputation grew with that of the magazine. In the Greenwich Village neighborhood where he and Althea lived in often-interrupted union, he moved smoothly and eagerly in the social and literary circles favored by his *New Yorker* colleagues, for most of whom Althea had a disdain that was returned in kind. From their acquaintance back in Paris, William Shirer remembers Althea as "what Jim would call a very 'bourgeois girl,' very middle class . . . , and Jim was – well, he noticed pretty girls, as did we all, and frequented a lot of bohemian-like places." Althea was not averse to artistic companions. She simply liked a different group of people and preferred spending time with them rather than with Thurber's friends – or Thurber.[21]

Thurber, although given to moodiness, could be a charming, sociable drinker who was interested in many things and delighted in arguing about all of them. He was infectiously amusing, a "man with one eye who could draw Early Woman, act like a Scottie, go into a fit over a no-hit-no-run dice baseball game," as Katharine Angell, soon to be E. B. White's wife, wrote to White in 1929. "There should be more Thurbers around."[22] He enjoyed imitating W. C. Fields or Ed Wynn, mimicking Harold Ross, or recreating the character of Jeeter Lester from Erskine Caldwell's "Tobacco Road." He sang sentimental tunes, especially of a melancholy sort ("Bye-Bye Blackbird" was his signature song), or such obscure ditties as "She'll Be True to Him in Monkey Doodle Town." He loved complicated anagrams and other word games, was a "running commentator and mine of information on every subject under the sun," as another friend recalled, and performed selections from a vast, entertaining repertoire of elaborate stories and anecdotes, polished to a fine sheen by repeated telling.[23] He relished practical jokes and was sufficiently secure in his self-esteem by now to make an unnerving jest out of his partial blindness.

"He had a wonderful sense of humor about his sightlessness," recalls Al Hirschfeld, *The New York Times*'s incomparable theatrical caricaturist since 1927. "He had a glass eye . . . and he used to change it at parties," Hirschfeld remembers with a chuckle, saying that Thurber kept a series of artificial eyes in reserve for this prank. As the evening wore on, Thurber's glass eye "became more bloodshot . . . , and at about two o'clock in the morning, he'd put one in, and it would be a little American flag! It was a shocker, you know. You'd look at him and there's a little American flag flying there in his eye."[24]

Although he may have been the life of some parties, Thurber's life at home was troubled. He and Althea were increasingly incompatible, and the tensions and woes of their marriage were mirrored in his stories of the period. Many of them are exquisitely crafted, often pointed miniatures of marital turmoil between a bumbling, put-upon husband and his efficient, dominating wife. The man is an idiot with anything mechanical, a romantic daydreamer who is easily flustered and frequently childlike; the woman is pretty, calculating, crisply authoritative, often condescending, sometimes flippant. They were Thurber and Althea.[25]

Before she went away, little Mrs. Monroe had led her husband from room to room, pointing out what was to go into storage and what was to be sent to the summer place in Connecticut. It was all quite simple, she told him. Apparently John Monroe hadn't been listening, however, for now, as he walked restlessly from room to room, picking up vases and putting them down again, he found he wasn't sure about anything. He wasn't sure about the china and glassware, for one thing. He stood and stared at them, trying to remember what it was his wife had said. All that he could recall was that she had spoken in the slow, precise way in which she always spoke to him in a crisis, as if he were a little deaf or feeble-minded. He decided, finally, that the glassware and china went into storage. Then he decided that they didn't. . . .

[The moving men] set to work so fast that three tables and a bed were down the stairs and onto the sidewalk before Mr. Monroe could say anything. Well, he was pretty sure about the great big pieces of furniture, anyway – they must go to storage. Great big pieces of furniture were always stored – that's why storage warehouses were so big. Mr. Monroe began to feel that he was getting a grip on the situation. "What about the china, chief?" one of the men asked him. Mr. Monroe hesitated. "Pack it and let it stand a while," he said, at last. "I want to think about it." From downstairs later he could hear the voices of the men, huge, sweating, rough fellows, joking about him: "This guy wants to think it over – ja get that, Joe?" Mr. Monroe's indecision and evident nervousness began to show up in the movers' attitude toward him. The "chief" and "mister" with which they had first addressed him changed to "buddy" and "mister" and finally, as Mr. Monroe strove desperately for an air of dignity and authority, to "sonny." [26]

*   *   *

"My husband," said little Mrs. Monroe, "is a collector."

This statement surprised no one more than Mr. Monroe, who was not a collector.

"And what do you collect, Mr. Monroe?" asked Mrs. Armsby, politely.

"Handkerchiefs," said Mrs. Monroe. "He collects handkerchiefs."

It was apparent to Mr. Monroe that his wife's remarkable statements were the unfortunate result of their having attended a cocktail party before dropping in, late, at Mrs. Armsby's. The teas which Mrs. Armsby gave on Sundays were the sort at which tea is served. The people who attend them did not attend cocktail parties, which were events almost as alien to their experience as the murders in the Rue Morgue. . . . The Monroes were quite young. The others were quite middle-aged and, up to this point, had been discussing the stock market.

"My husband also collects pencils," said Mrs. Monroe. It was warm in the room. The closeness of the air had, as it were, "got to" Mrs. Monroe. One saw this. Fortunately, not more than one – Mr. Monroe – saw this, for to the others there was no relationship between the atmosphere and the odd direction the small talk had thus suddenly taken.

"Indeed?" said Mrs. Penwarden.

"My husband has eight hundred and seventy-four thousand pencils," said Mrs. Monroe. . . .

Mr. Monroe was aware that his wife was alluding in a fanciful and distressingly untimely manner to a habit of his, which was to bring home from the office several pencils each day and to leave them on his desk, or failing that, on her dressing table. She frequently spoke to him disapprovingly about such things. For example, he had an unfortunate predilection for leaving towels on her dressing table, too. . . .

"It must be interesting to collect pencils," said Mr. Penwarden.

"My husband collects towels, too," said Mrs. Monroe. . . .[27]

When not in Manhattan, Thurber and Althea divided their time between two countryside retreats, one a well-known artistic community in Westport, Connecticut, which Althea preferred; the other, a farm in Westchester County, New York, rented by a group of *New Yorker* staffers whose company Thurber liked better. Often he and Althea went separately to the places they favored. Althea enjoyed flirting with the literary solons in Westport; Thurber developed a longstanding, often tempestuous relationship with Ann Honeycutt, a vivacious blond Southerner he met at the Westchester farm who was friendly – indeed, romantically involved – with a number of other *New Yorker* writers over the years. Thurber maintained an on-and-off romance and association with her for the rest of his life, although he wrote to E. B. White in 1952 that she had concluded, correctly, that he really didn't like her.

"She is right and I have figured out why. Our love never ripened into friendship." [28]

Thurber had other extramarital flings, but he and Althea remained married and by 1929 had reached a sort of modus vivendi: They rented a house near Westport, where she could be near her friends and raise dogs, an animal for which she shared Thurber's extravagant fondness; he lived for the most part in New York hotels, visiting Connecticut whenever loneliness or remorse got the better of him.

His literary output that year was considerable. In addition to five Mr. and Mrs. Monroe stories, he wrote "Talk of the Town" satires of the popular self-improvement books of the day and spoofed Fowler's *Dictionary of Modern English Usage,* Ross's favorite book: "Word has somehow got around that a split infinitive is always wrong. This is of a piece with the sentimental and outworn notion that it is always wrong to strike a lady." [29] In all, he produced twenty-seven casuals for *The New Yorker* in 1929, and his apprenticeship under White was proving both professionally fulfilling and personally enriching. He learned from White but did not copy him.

White was observing not only Thurber's literary development but his compulsive doodling as well. Thurber drew everywhere, on reams of yellow copy paper, on the desks, on the wastepaper baskets, on the floor, and on the walls, where his strange figures often were accompanied by enigmatic graffiti, such as the words "too late," sometimes separated by long distances or corners so someone spotting it would first see "too" and then, many inches or feet away, "late." (The drawings that somehow survived long enough to challenge the conservators from Stoneledge feature football players, fierce dogs, and a self-portrait that, unlike most of Thurber's wall-scribblings, he actually signed.) He dashed off the drawings at an astonishing rate, often completing one in less than a minute, and an equally astonishing number of them struck White as not only funny but brilliant, as pertinent and sometimes surreal snapshots of the conflicts between men and women, the sensitive superiority of dogs, the unsettling moments in social situations, and otherwise inexplicable events.

One of Thurber's innumerable pencil sketches particularly delighted White. It depicted a seal sitting on a rock, peering at two tiny spots in the distance and muttering, "Hm, explorers." White applied ink to Thurber's penciled lines and handed the drawing in to the regular Tuesday afternoon meeting of the magazine's art arbiters, who swiftly rejected it. The art editor, Rea Irvin (creator of *The New Yorker*'s trademark, the bemonocled dandy Eustace Tilley), was baffled by the crude submission and responded by sketching an anatomically correct seal's head on the drawing and returning it to White with the note: "This is the way a seal's whiskers go." White, undaunted, sent the drawing back with his own note: "This is the way a Thurber seal's whiskers go." It was rejected just as promptly the second time, and Thurber, absent-mindedly, threw it away.[30]

White persisted. He continued to apply ink to Thurber's drawings and send them to the weekly art meeting. Thurber, a bit disheartened by the constant rejections, thought he might have better luck if he spent a little more time on the drawings. He started to gussy them up with cross-hatching and shading. White intervened. "Don't do that," he advised. "If you ever got good you'd be mediocre."[31]

Ross, for his part, was scornful. He asked Thurber, "How the hell did you get the idea that you could *draw?*"[32]

White would not be deterred. When he and Thurber discovered that they were writing independent spoofs of the turgid, psychological sex tomes then being published, such as Dr. Joseph Collins's book *The*

43

Doctor Looks at Love and Life, they decided to pool their parodies, and White insisted that Thurber illustrate the combined text. Thurber obliged by scribbling thirty or forty drawings one evening. An editor at Harper and Brothers to whom they showed Thurber's drawings looked at them quizzically and said, "These, I take it, are the rough sketches from which the drawings will be produced?" White blithely replied, "No, these are the drawings themselves." Harper's swallowed hard and published the collaborative satire, *Is Sex Necessary? or Why You Feel The Way You Do,* in November 1929, replete with Thurber's drawings, unalloyed.[33] It was a roaring success (which few things were in the wake of the October 1929 Stock Market crash). It ridiculed pop psychoanalysis while kidding the conventions of modern courting rituals and matrimony; it was remarkably free of anything lewd, given its subject; and even more amazingly, it remains in print today, more than six decades after its publication, an extraordinary tribute to the quality of its humor, both in the prose and in the pictures.

In his "Note on the Drawings in This Book," White made the first attempt, and one of the most perceptive, to explain the seemingly artless figures that became known as "the Thurber man" and "the Thurber woman."

"When one studies the drawings, it soon becomes apparent that a strong undercurrent of grief runs through them. In almost every instance the man in the picture is badly frightened, or even hurt. These 'Thurber men' have come to be recognized as a distinct type in the world of art; they are frustrated, fugitive beings; at times they seem vaguely striving to get out of something without being seen (a room, a situation, a state of mind), at other times they are merely perplexed and too humble, or weak to move. The *women,* you will notice, are quite different: temperamentally they are much better adjusted to their surroundings than are the men, and mentally they are much less capable of making themselves uncomfortable."[34]

A few years later White added, in another supposedly mock but actually incisive analysis of Thurber's drawings: "He is the one artist I have ever known, capable of expressing, in a single drawing, physical embarrassment during emotional strain. That is, it is always apparent to Thurber that at the very moment one's heart is caught in an embrace, one's foot may be caught in a piano stool."[35]

Dorothy Parker also saw the poignancy underlying many of Thurber's cartoons; even his enraged characters have "a touching quality," she wrote. Yet as she also memorably observed, they all "have the outer semblance of unbaked cookies." The frumpish women "are of a dowdiness so overwhelming that it becomes tremendous style," and "the Thurber man, those deplorably *désoigné* Thurber men, would ask no better."[36]

And while Thurber's people seemed born of unbaked dough, his inimitable dogs originated in a childhood fascination with an aged lithograph of the Duke of Westminster's hunting hounds that hung in the front hallway of his grandfather's home in Columbus. Thurber began drawing his sad-eyed hounds around the age of six, and by the time he reached maturity he had developed a breed that "does not want to hunt anybody or anything," he wrote. His dog "loves serenity and heavy dinners, and wishes they would go on forever, like the brook."[37]

Whether human or canine, all of the characters Thurber drew were rendered with a remarkable economy of line that conveyed subtle expressions. A dot here, a centimeter of ink there, and full, intense emotions were evoked, or movement, graceful or awkward, was depicted. In the view of Al Hirschfeld, Thurber drew "like most writers" draw. He cited as other examples the simple but captivating sketches of Edward

Lear, nonsense poet nonpareil, and Clarence Day, whose memoirs of his "life with father" appeared in *The New Yorker* before they became a book and a play. "Lear and other writers who drew, they all seemed to draw the same way," Hirschfeld said. "They managed to keep that childlike creativity in their line." [38]

Others (Thurber not among them) thought Thurber's drawings had more sophistication than simplicity, and even saw a likeness between his work and that of the giants of modern art. Dorothy Parker, perhaps with tongue slightly in cheek, noted the "shy kinship" between Thurber's "boneless, loppy beings" and "the men and women of Picasso's later drawings, so truly and gratifyingly decorative." British painter and critic Paul Nash seriously likened Thurber's drawings to those of Matisse, and in time Nash's judgment was garbled by some newspapers on this side of the Atlantic, where it was written that Thurber was Matisse's favorite American artist. Thurber was uneasy about such accolades, and with reason: When he visited London in 1937 at a time when Matisse also happened to be there, the owner of a gallery where Thurber's drawings were on display tried to set up a meeting between Thurber and his supposed admirer. A secretary for Matisse icily responded that the master knew nothing of Thurber. A friend of Thurber's reported after World War II, however, that when he met Matisse in 1946 and asked him to name the best artist in the United States, the aged painter replied, "Monsieur Toobay." When his puzzled visitor asked Matisse how to spell the mysterious Toobay's name, the artist wrote "Thurber." [39]

Regardless of whether Matisse had ever heard of Thurber in the early 1930s, Harold W. Ross knew who he was, and Ross was baffled and frustrated that a staff member whose drawings he had rejected was now a celebrated cartoonist – and being published by someone else. He went into Thurber's office and glumly asked for "that goddam seal drawing." Told that it had been discarded casually upon repeated rejections, Ross exploded, "Well, don't throw things away just because I reject them! Do it again."[40]

Thurber dawdled until December 1931 before trying, and when he did, he later claimed, the rock on which the seal was supposed to repose turned out to look more like the head of a bed. So he completed the bed, put a bewildered man and annoyed woman in it, and had her saying: "All right, have it your way – you heard a seal bark." The cartoon's publication in *The New Yorker* of January 30, 1932, elicited "a truly ecstatic telegram from Bob Benchley," Thurber recalled, "than whom there was nobody whose praise a cartoonist or humorist would rather have had." Thurber gave Benchley the original drawing in appreciation, and Ross thereafter considered Thurber an established *New Yorker* artist.[41]

The Seal in the Bedroom (which would later become the title of Thurber's first book of cartoons) actually was not the first of his drawings to appear in *The New Yorker*. Capitalizing on Thurber's sudden fame as an illustrator as well as co-author of *Is Sex Necessary?*, Ross published some Thurber cartoons in 1930 to illustrate Thurber's antic parody of a column of pet advice appearing in the *New York Evening Post*, his old newspaper, and in many other papers then. In one Pet Department entry, under a drawing of a dog lying rigid, flat on its back, its eyes closed, its legs sticking straight up in the air, and its tail stretched out, Thurber presented an improbable question and answer:

Q. I enclose a sketch of the way my dog William has been lying for two days now. I think there must be something wrong with him. Can you tell me how to get him out of this?   Mrs. L.L.G.

A. I should judge from the drawing that William is in a trance. Trance states, however, are rare with dogs. It may just be ecstasy. If at the end of another twenty-four hours he doesn't seem to be getting anywhere, I should give him up. The position of the ears leads me to believe that he may be enjoying himself in a quiet way, but the tail is somewhat alarming.[42]

By 1931, Thurber was ready to publish a book all his own, *The Owl in the Attic and Other Perplexities,* featuring the Pet Department as well as the eight Monroe stories, and illustrated with his cartoons.

Unlike his meticulous method of writing, which sometimes involved slow, repeated revisions and fine-tuning of troublesome pieces, Thurber's drawings were produced in such a slapdash manner and given away so casually that, as he wrote to a friend, "It seems that at times I have drawn as many as thirty pictures for drunken ladies at drunken parties, drunken ladies whom I had never seen before but who now pop up here and there and remind me of our old intimacy."[43]

The cartoons he did for publication did not take any more time to draw. Frequently he would just start drawing and allow whatever turned up on the paper to suggest the subject. Then he would compose the caption. The ideas for his drawings, however spontaneous, often echo deep, occasionally dark emotions. Insanity, infidelity, and mayhem are often found in Thurber's cartoon world, as in ours. Women almost invariably are depicted disparagingly as overbearing or fatuous; the men often are seen as worried, ineffectual, and put-upon.

The animals in his drawings – particularly the dogs – seem more civilized than the humans. In "Memorial," a touching tribute to his first poodle, Thurber makes clear that he found dogs more dependable, sensible, and sane than humans. His dog, he wrote, "tried patiently at all times to understand Man's way of life: the rolling of his wheels;

the raising of his voice; the ringing of his bells; his way of searching out with lights the dark protecting corners of the night; his habit of building his beds inside walls, high above the nurturing earth." His cartoon dog, Thurber told one interviewer, was "a sound creature in a crazy world."[44]

E. B. White firmly believed that Thurber's drawings were greater works of genius than his writings, but Thurber himself refused to accord his artwork much honor. He was annoyed when his drawings received more attention than his prose, and he liked to tell the story of how another *New Yorker* cartoonist, incensed at having a drawing rejected, bellowed at Ross: "Why do you reject drawings of mine, and print stuff by that fifth-rate artist Thurber?"

" 'Third-rate,' said Ross, coming promptly and bravely to the defense of my stature as an artist and his own reputation as an editor," Thurber wrote in *The Years with Ross*.[45]

By the time Thurber went completely blind in the 1940s, he had published 307 captioned cartoons in *The New Yorker*, and Ross was distressed at the thought that no more stringy-haired Thurber women, elastic, bald-headed Thurber men, or solemn Thurber dogs would appear in the magazine's pages. Thurber sought to console him. "If I couldn't write, I couldn't breathe," he wrote to Ross, "but giving up drawing is only a little worse than giving up tossing cards in a hat. I once flipped in forty-one out of the whole deck, at twelve feet."[46]

Although Thurber's professional life was booming by 1931, his private affairs remained murky. A reconciliation with the intermittently estranged Althea resulted in the purchase of an old farmhouse and twenty acres of land in Sandy Hook, Connecticut, as well as the birth of their daughter, Rosemary, on October 6, 1931.

"I know there was at least one other woman in my father's life" at

49

that time, Rosemary Thurber says now. He had once again left Althea, but she "had called and said she heard somebody on the stairs and she was scared, so he went over – I don't even know where this happened – and that was the night I was conceived. . . . I think he was on the verge of moving in with somebody else."[47]

Indeed, just prior to the night of Rosemary's birth Thurber and Althea quarreled, and he was spending the evening with his old girlfriend Ann Honeycutt when his daughter was born. Rosemary's birth, not surprisingly, prompted another reconciliation with Althea. At first an apprehensive, diffident father, he would become a devoted, even indulgent parent. "I never, ever remember him being angry at me or yelling," Rosemary says. "He was just sort of, probably, too good to be true; always pleasant."[48]

He was not happy, however, as a husband. More and more of his time was spent with other women and away from his Sandy Hook home. He stayed in Manhattan, living in hotels, tossing his dirty clothes onto towering piles in the closets, pub-crawling and party-hopping all night, writing from dawn until exhaustion overcame him. He was now a dedicated, heavy drinker, prone to bursts of anger and combativeness. Charming, warm, and kind when sober, he became increasingly argumentative and might erupt in unexpected fury after the third or fourth round of Scotch, smashing glassware or furniture, lashing out verbally, sometimes even physically, at friends. Some years later, Thurber would grimly describe himself at parties as "that tall, wild-eyed son of a bitch, with hair in his eyes, a glass in his hand, screaming and vilifying."[49] Elliott Nugent, likening a Thurber tirade's effect to that of a hurricane on a sailboat, noted that calm – and contrition – always followed the storm. "Next day, while you are patching your sails and cutting away wreckage, Thurber appears in a canoe, bearing fruit and flowers."

" 'Was I bad last night?' he mutters, with a sheepish smile.

"Too weak to hurl your last broken harpoon, you invite him aboard and borrow his ukelele."[50]

Females often were the targets of Thurber's wrath, whether they were the wives of friends, other women he knew well, or innocent strangers. Fame, which he had wanted dearly, proved a mixed blessing. Sometimes he did not handle it well. Hobart (Hobey) Weekes, an early editor at *The New Yorker,* once told Heywood Hale Broun about an incident in the small lobby of the Algonquin Hotel when some young ladies from Columbus had their adulation for Thurber sorely tested, if not shattered.

"Apparently there was at one time . . . a glass screen in the lobby of the Algonquin for the purpose of shutting the noise of the dining room out from the drinkers in the lobby," Broun said, recalling Weekes's anecdote. "Hobey and Thurber were sitting at one of the little tables in the lobby drinking and two young women came up to Thurber and said, 'Oh, Mr. Thurber, would you sign our cocktail napkins? We are from Columbus, too.' And Thurber snarled at them to get lost, and they said, 'Oh, we've been to theater, and it would be just so perfect if would you sign our napkins.' And Thurber picked up the telephone on the table and threw it through the glass wall, causing a great shattering collapse of crystal, and said, 'Have I convinced you?' At which point, sobbing, they ran out of the Algonquin."

"Now, I was not present at the destruction of the glass wall," Broun added, "but Hobey was a man of great journalistic honesty, and I'm inclined to believe him, and it's more or less in the character of Thurber."[51]

No one knew the nature of that character better than Thurber himself. Self-centered though he may have been, he also was painfully self-aware. In the poignant story "One Is a Wanderer," his lonely, achingly familiar protagonist roams midtown Manhattan on a cold Sunday in February, reflecting on his solitary life, on the good times he and one woman had spent with a second couple, and then, over brandy in a hotel lobby, he thinks of how another woman now scolds him when he drinks too much.

It would be gloomy and close in his hotel room, and his soiled shirts would be piled on the floor of the closet where he had been flinging them for weeks, where he had been flinging them for months, and his papers would be disarranged on the tops of the tables and on the desk, and his pipes would be lying around, the pipes he had smoked determinedly for a while only to give them up, as he always did, to go back to cigarettes. He turned into the street leading to his hotel, walking slowly, trying to decide what to do with the night. He had too many nights alone. Once he had enjoyed being alone. Now it was hard to be alone. He couldn't read anymore, or write, at night. Books he tossed aside after nervously flipping through them; the writing he tried to do turned into spirals and circles and squares and empty faces. . . .

He had several brandies . . . in the lobby and began to think about calling up people. He thought of the Graysons. He saw the Graysons, not as they would be, sitting in their apartment, close together and warmly, but as he and Lydia had seen them in another place and another year. The four had shared a bright vacation once. He remembered various attitudes and angles and lights and colors of that vacation. There is something about four people, two couples, that like each other and get along, that have a swell time; that grow in intimacy and understanding. One's life is made up of twos, and of fours. The Graysons understood the nice little arrangements of living, the twos and fours. Two is company, four is a party, three is a crowd. One is a wanderer.

. . . Look here now, he told himself, you're getting too cockeyed now; you're getting into one of those states, you're getting into one of those states that Marianne keeps telling you about, one of those states when people don't like to have you around. . . . Marianne, he thought. He went back to his chair, ordered another brandy, and thought about Marianne.

She doesn't know how I start my days, he thought, she only knows how I end them. She doesn't know how I started my life. She only knows me when night gets me. If I could only be the person she wants me to be. . . . I wouldn't get mad suddenly, about nothing. I wouldn't snarl at nice people. About what she says is nothing. I wouldn't be "unbearable." Her word "unbearable." A female word, female as a cat. Well, she's right, too. I am unbearable. "George," he said to the waiter, "I am unbearable, did you know that?" "No, sir, I did not, sir," said the waiter. "I would not call you unbearable, Mr. Kirk." "Well, you don't know, George," he said. "It just happens that I am unbearable. It just happened that way. It's a long story." "Yes, sir," said the waiter.[52]

On many occasions, when Thurber was just the opposite of unbearable, he was full of hilarious stories about his bizarre relatives and peculiar childhood and adolescence – stories he told by acting out all the parts with professional skill. Inevitably, he put many of these tales, polished by performance, into writing, published them in *The New Yorker* during 1933, and compiled them in the book *My Life and Hard Times,* which came out in November of that year.

Expressing the view of many critics, Burton Bernstein has called *My Life and Hard Times* Thurber's "best work, best because it is unadulterated Thurber at the height of his unique literary and graphic invention. He equalled the prose and pictures of *My Life and Hard Times* in many later individual efforts, but never again was there a single series on one theme so immaculate."[53]

Like the "Days" books, those artful, fiction-embellished memoirs that many consider H. L. Mencken's greatest work, Thurber's supposed recollections of his family and their adventures are as much fantasy as fact. (Mencken, once berated by a newspaper colleague for inventing anecdotes about their early days as reporters, cheerfully admitted doing so. "It makes a better story," he said.) That the years of which

Thurber wrote, the period from 1900 to World War I, are now so distant does not diminish the delight readers find in these stories. Individual eccentricities, familial misunderstandings, public absurdities, and educational inanities all know no era; they are timeless. The book has never gone out of print.

The Thurber family he depicts is awash in idiosyncrasies and revels in confusion. Thurber once defined humor as "emotional chaos told about calmly and quietly in retrospect," and in *My Life and Hard Times,* his stories of the incidents in which chaos overcame his family, and Columbus, all are recounted with a face as straight and placid as Buster Keaton's. "The Night the Bed Fell" is, like the equally chaotic "The Day the Dam Broke," a story about the overwrought reactions to events which, the titles notwithstanding, actually did not happen: The bed didn't fall; the dam didn't break.[54]

In fact, according to Thurber's brother Robert, their father sometimes did sleep in the attic of their home, and once the bed up there did collapse on him, but from that seed of truth sprouted Thurber's wild, fanciful account of the escalating misunderstandings and irrationality attendant on his mother's mistaken belief that the attic bed had fallen on his father.

Father retires to the attic "to be away where he could think" (a quirky rationale not otherwise explained), and mother fears that the wobbly old bed with its massive headboard might fall apart and kill him. Around 2 A.M., the Army cot on which Thurber is sleeping overturns with a crash, mother awakes in the next room, certain that father has been bludgeoned by the collapsing headboard, and cries, "Let's go to your poor father!" One of Thurber's brothers, believing mother has become hysterical for no reason, repeatedly shouts, "You're all right, Mamma!" A visiting cousin who lives in dread of suffocating in his sleep, awakes, thinks he is dying, and douses himself with spirits of camphor. Nearly overcome by the smelling salts, he smashes out a window for air as Thurber, underneath the overturned cot, yells, "Get me out of this!" Mother frantically pulls on the stuck attic door while Thurber's other brother shouts questions at her and the family dog barks up a storm. Thurber and his cousin finally make their way to the attic door, the dog lunges at the cousin, whom he never liked, and father, baffled and groggy, at last emerges from the attic to ask, "What in the name of God is going on here?" When the wacky sequence of events eventually is "put together like a gigantic jigsaw puzzle," mother finds solace in the fact that the family's cantankerous, delusional grandfather wasn't witness to the brouhaha. The grandfather in *My Life and Hard Times*, unlike the redoubtable William M. Fisher, flits in and out of a fantasy world in which the Civil War still rages and Columbus policemen become deserters from General Meade's army.

"The Day the Dam Broke" also had its genesis in fact. There was indeed a flood in March 1913 that inundated the west side of Columbus, and a panicked populace on the east side did flee when rumors ran rampant that the Scioto River dam had broken, but Thurber's account of the panic is full of fictional people and absurd events created to enhance the lunacy of what really happened. Thurber liked to say that what he wrote was reality "twisted to the right into humor rather than to the left into tragedy." [55]

The acclaim for *My Life and Hard Times* was instant and impressive. No less a personage than Ernest Hemingway offered a suitably amusing blurb for the book: "Even when Thurber was writing under the name of Alice B. Toklas, we knew he had it in him if he could only get it out." The reception accorded the book by Thurber's family, however, was decidedly mixed. At first neither Thurber's mother nor father enjoyed the celebrity they now had by virtue of their fictionalized selves — especially because some of the goofiness attributed to them and their family was all too true. Thurber's father *was* baffled by anything mechanical; his mother *did* set out tidbits for the household's mice along with food for the regular pets; his grandmother *had* "lived the latter years of her life in the horrible suspicion that electricity was dripping all over the house . . . [leaking] out of empty sockets if the wall switch had been left on." And he *did* have an aunt "who never went to bed at night without the fear that a burglar was going to get in and blow chloroform under her door with a tube. To avert this calamity — for she was in greater dread of anesthetics than of losing her household goods — she always piled her money, silverware, and other valuables in a neat stack just outside her bedroom with a note reading: 'This is all I have. Please take it and do not use your chloroform, as this is all I have.' "[56]

In no way funny, but equally true, was the further deterioration of Thurber's already half-dissolved marriage. "I think they had other interests, other friends," says Rosemary Thurber. "I don't know how much basis they had for a good relationship to start with. . . . My father once said to me that it was all his fault . . . , and of course I don't buy that. . . . Nothing is ever all one person's fault."[57]

Thurber's visits to Sandy Hook became increasingly infrequent, and he was involved with more women in Manhattan, including his long-time inamorata, Ann Honeycutt. Ironically, it was at a party at Honey-cutt's Greenwich Village apartment, late in 1929, that Thurber met Helen Muriel Wismer, a respected editor of pulp fiction magazines, who would become his second wife. The daughter of a Congregationalist minister and a graduate of Mount Holyoke, she had a fine literary sense and was a witty, engaging conversationalist. She recalled that on their first significant date, Thurber declaimed virtually all of *My Life and Hard Times*, which he then was writing. She was enthralled. They continued dating, but she considered marriage an unlikely development; the competition from other women seemed too intense.[58]

As far as Althea was concerned, the game was over. In the summer of 1934, she told Thurber she wanted a legal separation, and hired a lawyer to work out the details. Thurber was reasonable and cooperative, having his own attorney draft a liberal agreement that granted custody of Rosemary to Althea, gave her the Sandy Hook property, the family insurance policies, alimony and child support, plus Thurber's advance royalties from *My Life and Hard Times*.[59]

Within a few weeks, Althea filed for divorce. Since Connecticut law then made divorces difficult to obtain, she cited "intolerable cruelty" as the reason for their breakup, and Thurber winced at the prospects of a thoroughly unpleasant proceeding. His drinking increased and his creative productivity diminished. One of the few drawings he did at this time was one of his most misogynist, and memorable. Captioned "Home," it depicts a tiny, cowering man approaching a large house that dissolves into the form of a gigantic, glowering woman. Early in 1935, Thurber went to a sanitarium in upstate New York to sober up.

When he returned to New York, Thurber spent more and more time with Ann Honeycutt, but she also was dating St. Clair McKelway, a colleague of Thurber's at *The New Yorker*, and decided to marry him. Thurber was shaken, and then had to face the publicity surrounding his divorce from Althea in May 1935. In order to justify the claim of intolerable cruelty, counsel for Althea sought to magnify Thurber's admittedly erratic behavior. Althea testified that he was prone to violence, unconcerned about his baby, financially unsupportive, and repeatedly unfaithful. The tabloid press lapped it up, and even the *Columbus Sunday Star* ran a splashy account under the headline "Was Sex Necessary To Jim Thurber?" His family in Columbus was mortified.[60]

The day following Thurber's divorce, he met Helen Wismer in the lobby of the Algonquin for an after-work drink and promptly proposed to her. After retiring to the ladies' room to get a grip on herself, Helen returned to the lobby and just as promptly said yes. They were married on June 25, 1935, a month to the day after Thurber's divorce from Althea.

Harold Ross had worried that a happy marriage might dilute the acid in Thurber's corrosively comic depictions of marital discord. He even enlisted Robert Benchley's reluctant assistance in an effort to persuade Thurber that a quick remarriage might not be a good thing. Both Ross and Benchley soon came to regret their well-intentioned meddling. They took an instant liking to Helen and said that she was well-suited to help – and handle – the personal and financial tangles of their often-troubled friend.[61]

And the battles between the men and women in Thurber's stories showed no signs of abating, as "A Couple of Hamburgers" amply demonstrated:

It had been raining for a long time, a slow, cold rain falling out of iron-colored clouds. They had been driving since morning and they still had a hundred and thirty miles to go. It was about three o'clock in the afternoon. "I'm getting hungry," she said. He took his eyes off the wet, winding road for a fraction of a second and said, "We'll stop at a dog-wagon." She shifted her position irritably. "I wish you wouldn't call them *dog*-wagons," she said. He pressed the klaxon button and went around a slow car. "That's what they are," he said. "Dog-wagons." She waited a few seconds. "*Decent* people call them *diners*," she told him, and added, "Even if you call them diners, I don't like them." He speeded up a hill. "They have better stuff than most restaurants," he said. "Anyway, I want to get home before dark and it takes too long in a restaurant. We can stay our stomachs with a couple of hamburgers." She lighted a cigarette and he asked her to light one for him. She lighted one deliberately and handed it to him. "I wish you wouldn't say 'stay our stomachs'," she said. "You know I hate that. It's like 'sticking to your ribs.' You say that all the time." He grinned. . . . They drove on for several miles without a word; he kept chortling every now and then.

"What's that funny sound," she asked suddenly. It invariably made him angry when she heard a funny sound. "What funny sound?" he demanded. "You're always hearing funny sounds." She laughed briefly. "That's what you said when the bearing burned out," she reminded him. "I noticed it, all right," he said. "Yes," she said. "When it was too late." She enjoyed bringing up the subject of the burned-out bearing whenever he got to chortling. "It was too late when *you* noticed it, as far as that goes," he said. Then, after a pause, "Well, what does it sound like *this* time? All engines make a noise running, you know." "I know all about that," she answered. "It sounds like — it sounds like a lot of safety pins being jiggled around in a tumbler." He snorted. "That's your imagination. Nothing gets the matter with a car that sounds like a lot of safety pins. I happen to know that." She tossed away her cigarette. "Oh, sure," she said. "You always happen to know everything." They drove on in silence.[62]

If anything, a return to domestic tranquility, or at least a semblance of it, revitalized Thurber creatively. He was entering one of the most productive periods of his life, fueled, perhaps, by a presentiment that he and the printed page might soon part company.

4

The Kingdom of the Partly Blind

Thurber and Helen led a hectic life in Manhattan. They moved into a furnished apartment on Fifth Avenue, where Thurber did most of his writing. He visited *The New Yorker*'s offices for amusement, drank with friends at his favorite pubs, Bleeck's and Costello's (once drawing an elaborate pencil mural on the wall of the latter that is still there), then went home so he and Helen could head out for social engagements or entertain guests themselves. They got little sleep.[1]

Somehow Thurber did get a lot of work done, much of it superb. He finished a series of illustrations for a new compilation of previously published pieces, which came out late in 1935 under the title *The Middle-Aged Man on the Flying Trapeze*. It remains a remarkable demonstration of Thurber's multifaceted talent, containing some of his finest satires, parodies, explorations of sexual and psychological conflicts, and reminiscences of his youth in Columbus. Thurber's personal favorite in the collection was his first great wordplay piece, "The Black Magic of Barney Haller," the tale of an immigrant hired man who seems to travel with his own personal thunderstorm and garbles the English language in a way that baffles – and frightens – Thurber. With his love of the murkiness in language and his keen ear for dialect, he made the story a masterpiece of misunderstanding.[2]

"Dis morning bime by," said Barney, "I go hunt grotches in de voods."

"That's fine," I said, and turned a page and pretended to be engrossed in what I was reading. Barney walked on; he had wanted to talk some more, but he walked on. After a paragraph or two, his words began to come between me and the words in the book. "Bime by I go hunt grotches in de voods." If you are susceptible to such things, it is not difficult to visualize grotches. They fluttered into my mind: ugly little creatures, about the size of whippoorwills, only covered with blood and honey and the scrapings of church bells. Grotches . . . Who and what, I wondered, really was this thing in the form of a hired man that kept anointing me ominously, in passing, with abracadabra?

The "grotches" turn out to be "crotches," or crotched saplings used as supports under the branches of fruit-laden peach trees, a simple enough explanation of what Barney Haller meant. But when he suggests the next evening that "We go to the garrick now and become warbs," Thurber will have nothing to do with it. He begins tossing Lewis Carroll nonsense at Barney as a sort of talisman against bewitchment.

"Listen!" I barked, suddenly. "Did you know that even when it isn't brillig I can produce slithy toves? Did you happen to know that the mome rath never lived that could outgrabe me? Yeah and furthermore I can become anything I want to; even if I were a warb, I wouldn't have to keep on being one if I didn't want to."

Barney backs away and never returns. He had meant to say he was going into the garret to get rid of some wasps, but no matter.[3] Among the other pieces in *The Middle-Aged Man on the Flying Trapeze* were the poignant but funny tale of Emma Inch, a peculiar, mousey cook who is terrified of hotels ("They burn down"), cab drivers ("They all take cocaine"), and the prospect of going to Martha's Vineyard with her aged dog; a devilish parody of a series in *Scribner's* magazine based on historical "what-ifs," such as "If Napoleon Had Escaped to America," with Thurber's hypothetical "If Grant Had Been Drinking at Appomattox" ending as the alcohol-befuddled Grant mistakenly surrenders his sword to General Lee; and a series of stories about "beaten husbands," all written during the final dismal months of his marriage to Althea.

Some modern readers might view Thurber's tales of abused husbands as hopelessly dated, since it may be unfashionable now to imply that any woman could be a harridan or any man might be henpecked. But no matter how antifeminist Thurber's work often was — and his misogyny seems undeniable — the human types that he created remain as vivid and true today as ever. Such individuals do exist; such interpersonal conflicts do occur; we all can recognize people we know in the stories he tells, or perhaps even see ourselves, heaven forbid. Consider Mr. Preble's attempt to get rid of his wife.

"I was going to hit you over the head with this shovel," said Mr. Preble.

"You were, huh?" said Mrs. Preble. "Well get that out of your mind. Do you want to leave a great big clue right here in the middle of everything where the first detective that comes snooping around will find it? Go out in the street and find some piece of iron or something -- something that doesn't belong to you."

"Oh, all right," said Mr. Preble. "But there won't be any piece of iron in the street. Women always expect to pick up a piece of iron anywhere."

"If you look in the right place you'll find it," said Mrs. Preble. "And don't be gone long. Don't you dare stop at the cigar store. I'm not going to stand down here in this cold cellar all night and freeze."

"All right," said Mr. Preble. "I'll hurry."

"And shut that *door* behind you!" she screamed after him. "Where were you born – in a barn?" [4]

Thurber concluded the collection in *Middle-Aged Man* with one of his more troubling psychological pieces, "A Box to Hide In," which deals with the quest of a fearful, neurotic man for the phantom safe haven of a huge box. Reviewers were impressed not only with the deftness of Thurber's light pieces but the dark undertones in others. He was, wrote one critic, "a Joyce in false-face" whose stories featured characters who "take their subconsciouses out on benders."[5]

During the first months of his marriage to Helen, Thurber also began work on a series of profiles for *The New Yorker* of one-time celebrities who had been lost, or sought refuge, in obscurity. These "Where Are They Now?" pieces, based on the research of other reporters on the magazine's staff and written under the pseudonym Jared L. Manley, are some of Thurber's finest nonfiction prose, and one of them actually set a legal precedent. Among his subjects was a former mathematical prodigy, William James Sidis, whose skills had amazed adult mathematicians when he was just eleven. The now-adult Sidis sued *The New Yorker,* claiming that his right to privacy had been violated. The case eventually reached the U.S. Supreme Court, which let stand a lower court's ruling that former public figures were still considered to be public figures legally and could be reported on as such.[6]

Other subjects Thurber wrote about in this twenty-four-part series included Virginia O'Hanlon, who as a child had written the letter to the *New York Sun* that prompted the immortal editorial reply, "Yes, Virginia, there is a Santa Claus"; John Joseph Killion, who as Jake Kilrain had boxed seventy-five rounds against John L. Sullivan; and Irvin Conn, who wrote "Yes! We Have No Bananas," a song Thurber personally despised. A number of the people profiled in the series had been central figures in once-notorious murder cases. Among them were Willie Stevens, the supposedly simple but cagey suspect acquitted of involvement in the formerly famous, still unsolved Hall-Mills double murder of 1922, and the principals involved in the 1912 gangland slaying of gambler Herman Rosenthal, including a quartet of hired killers with colorful noms de guerre – Lefty Louie, Gyp the Blood, Whitey Lewis, and Dago Frank.[7] Thurber had a fondness for grisly crimes, a peculiar taste not uncommon among old newspaper reporters.

In the late winter of 1936, the exhausted Thurbers decided to find a restful retreat and settled on Bermuda. There they became close friends of Ronald and Jane Williams, a young British couple who lived in Felicity Hall, the house in which Hervey Allen wrote *Anthony Adverse*. It was a working vacation for Thurber, and he liked to tell tourists who visited the old mansion that he was using Hervey Allen's desk to write *Anthony Adverse* backward.[8] Ronald Williams edited *Bermudian* magazine, and Thurber's fondness for the Williamses was such that he willingly wrote occasional pieces for the magazine for free. One evening during this visit to Bermuda, the Thurbers and Williamses met Sinclair Lewis, deep in his cups, and had a dinner with him that was marked by his swift changes from charming to churlish. Lewis expressed great admiration for Thurber's work, quoted extensive patches from it, and impressed Thurber as the "only drunken writer I have ever met who said nothing about his own work and praised that of another writer present."[9]

When the Thurbers returned to New York in the spring of 1936, they concluded that the fast life in Manhattan might be the death of them. They decided to give up their Fifth Avenue apartment and move to the countryside of northern Connecticut. Thurber remained under contract to *The New Yorker* but was able to free-lance elsewhere. One such piece was an admiring article he wrote for *Stage* magazine about *Tonight at Eight-Thirty*, a trio of one-act plays by Noel Coward, whom he and

Helen had met in Boston and liked immensely, even though Thurber envied Coward's seemingly effortless skills.[10]

That fall, during a trip to Columbus for Thanksgiving, the Thurbers encountered the poet Carl Sandburg, then on tour singing folk songs and strumming a guitar. At a reception following Sandburg's concert, he and Thurber drank, sang, and swapped stories far into the night. It was a memorable start to a lifelong friendship, conducted mostly through letters of mutual admiration and encouragement.[11]

The Thurbers settled in Litchfield, Connecticut, renting a three-bedroom house surrounded by tall maple and elm trees, just across the road from the birthplace of Harriet Beecher Stowe and hard by the birthplace of Ethan Allen. Thurber, ever the history buff, was delighted by the surroundings. Helen, unobtrusively efficient, smoothly took over management of Thurber's increasingly complicated professional life, seeing to it that his once-abysmal wardrobe of cheap suits and shabby ties became a model of understated good taste, succeeding in establishing a warm relationship with Rosemary, and somehow maintaining a cordial association, when necessary, with Althea.[12]

Thurber began work on some withering commentaries dissecting the spate of self-improvement books that were popular then as now. "I've had to read the most incredible crap," he wrote to a friend, including in that category Dale Carnegie's *How to Win Friends and Influence People,* Dr. James L. Mursell's *Streamline Your Mind,* David Seabury's *How to Worry Successfully,* and Dr. Louis E. Bisch's *Be Glad You're Neurotic.* The only thing that cheered Thurber was the obvious absurdity of so much within the self-help genre, which he delighted in demolishing. These *New Yorker* articles, combined with other stories and brief essays, became his next book, published in 1937 and entitled *Let Your Mind Alone! and Other More or Less Inspirational Pieces.*

Fulfilling a fantasy of every once-spurned writer, Thurber included dollops of the previously rejected *Why We Behave Like Microbe Hunters* in *Let Your Mind Alone!,* selling it to an unaware but now eager publisher, Harper, which had turned down the original when Thurber was unknown.[13]

Among the assorted "inspirational" pieces appended to the pop psychology items in *Let Your Mind Alone!* was Thurber's amusing yet touching description of the visual oddities he regularly encountered because of his poor eyesight, now reduced to about two-fifths of the vision in his one good eye without his eyeglasses, and worse than that at night even with them. In the 1936 piece "The Admiral on the Wheel," he wrote of the spectacular things he saw on the occasions when his glasses were broken and he ventured forth without them: "I saw the Cuban flag flying over a national bank, I saw a gay old lady with a gray parasol walk right through the side of a truck, I saw a cat roll across the street in a small striped barrel, I saw bridges rise lazily into the air like balloons."

And on a night-time drive with a friend, with his two-fifths vision working "a kind of magic in the night," Thurber yelled at the driver to stop the car because what he "didn't see and I did see . . . was a little old admiral in full-dress uniform riding a bicycle at right angles to the car I was in. He might have been starlight behind a tree or a billboard advertising Moxie; I don't know . . . , but I would recognize him if I saw him again."

I suppose you have to have just the right proportion of sight to encounter such phenomena. . . . With three-fifths vision or better, I suppose the Cuban flag would have been an American flag, the gay old lady a garbage man with a garbage can on his back, the cat a piece of butcher's paper blowing in the wind, the floating bridges smoke from tugs, hanging in the air. With perfect vision,

one is inextricably trapped in the workaday world, a prisoner of reality. . . .
For the hawk-eyed person life has none of those soft edges which for me blur
into fantasy. . . . The kingdom of the partly blind is a little like Oz, a little like
Wonderland, a little like Poictesme. Anything you can think of, and a lot you
never would think of, can happen there.[14]

The problem was that Thurber seemed perilously close to journeying
from the supposedly enchanting world of the partly blind into what for
him would be the terrifying realm of the sightless. For a number of years
he had experienced frightening episodes of near-total blindness; back
in 1928, he had stumbled into Katharine Angell's office at *The New
Yorker* late one night and asked if he could ride home with her because
he had suddenly lost the ability to see.[15] Seven years later he was forced
to give up driving at night, and his ophthalmologist, Dr. Gordon Bruce,
detected an incipient cataract in his good eye. By 1937, the cataract had
clouded the lens of his eye and an operation was called for, but Thurber,
knowing that a successful operation was at best in those days a fifty-
fifty proposition, decided to postpone the surgery in order to take an
extended trip to Europe and show its wonders to his wife.

In May 1937 they put their 1932 Ford V-8 aboard the *Ile de France*
and sailed for France. After a blissful tour of Normandy they drove to
Paris, where they found Hemingway, Dorothy Parker, Lillian Hellman,
Janet Flanner, and others eager to entertain them in cafés and argue
with Thurber, if the mood struck. The Spanish Civil War was raging,
and Thurber, though antifascist, felt that American writers would be
misguided to abandon their explorations of individual turmoil and pain
in order to go off to war. "Art does not rush to the barricades," he had
insisted a year earlier in a scathing review of an anthology of the writings of American Marxists.[16] One night he, Hemingway, and foreign
correspondent Vincent (Jimmy) Sheean debated with Ring Lardner's

son James, a young reporter, the question of whether Lardner should go to Spain to fight. Thurber was the only one advising the young Lardner to go as a correspondent, if need be, not as a combatant. Hemingway and Sheean were all for Lardner's going as a soldier. Young Lardner decided to enlist, and was killed in action. Nearly twenty years later, Thurber recalled sadly: "I was one of the last to plead with him in Paris not to go to Spain, but he just gave me the old Lardner smile. Hemingway and Jimmy Sheean were pulling against me." [17]

A show of Thurber's drawings opened in the spring of 1937 in London, the Thurbers' next stop. His work had always been popular in England, given the British fondness for things slightly balmy, and his reception there was enthusiastic and friendly. "The hallmark of sophistication," the *London Daily Sketch* proclaimed, "is to adore the drawings of James Thurber." [18] He reciprocated in kind, writing little pieces for English newspapers, granting interviews and even agreeing to a British Broadcasting Corporation request that he appear on an odd new medium called television and draw some pictures for the audience. Thurber wrote home to friends that the viewers saw everything he drew "clear as a bell." Later he covered some of the Davis Cup competition at Wimbledon for *The New Yorker* by watching a match on a ten-inch TV screen, which he likened to "a photograph in an album come to life." In London, he and Helen dined with Charles Laughton and Elsa Lancaster, met H. G. Wells, the movie producer Alexander Korda, and other creative lights, and had themselves a splendid time. [19] Thurber even was delighted that two of his drawings were stolen from the gallery where they were on display. He told an interviewer he was "pleased mightily that anybody would risk arrest . . . for stealing some of my drawings. After all, if you have your drawings stolen, you're made." [20]

In the summer they drove through Wales and Scotland; in September they went back to the Continent for further motoring through Holland

and France. A return to Paris in the fall led to a leisurely, sybaritic amble through the countryside toward the South of France, with stops at all the best hotels and restaurants.

Throughout their travels, Thurber wrote casuals for *The New Yorker.* In one, "There's No Place Like Home," he drolly described "the dark, cumulative power" of a pocket book of English-to-French phrases designed to help travelers weather "workaday disasters." He devised a short, imaginative scenario of horrors featuring the expressions in the book, *Collins' Pocket Interpreters: France,* which contained about three times as many phrases for use "when one is in trouble as when everything is going all right," Thurber wrote. "This, my own experience has shown, is about the right ratio, but God spare me from some of the difficulties for which the traveler is prepared in Mr. Collins' melancholy narrative poem." For example, in the section headed "At the Hotel," matters quickly "go from worse to awful":

"Did you not get my letter?" "I wrote to you three weeks ago." "I asked for a first-floor room." "If you can't give me something better, I shall go away." "The chambermaid never comes when I ring." "I cannot sleep at night, there is so much noise." "I have just had a wire. I must leave at once." Panic has begun to set in, and it is not appeased by the advent of "The Chambermaid": "Are you the chambermaid?" "There are no towels here." "The sheets on this bed are damp." "This room is not clean." "I have seen a mouse in the room." "You will have to set a mouse trap here." The bells of hell at this point begin to ring in earnest: "These shoes are not mine." "I put my shoes here, where are they now?" "The light is not good." "The bulb is broken." "The radiator is too warm." "The radiator doesn't work." "It is cold in this room." "This is not clean, bring me another." "I don't like this." "I can't eat this. Take it away!"[21]

The couple spent Thurber's forty-third birthday and Christmas in Italy, where the charm of Rome and Naples succeeded in tempering

Thurber's antipathy to Mussolini's Fascists. Early in the new year, he and Helen returned to France, settled in an inexpensive villa at Cap d'Antibes near Nice, and had a brief, memorable encounter with Winston Churchill, who was staying at the nearby seaside mansion of socialite Maxine Elliot. They were invited to a tea there at which the Duke and Duchess of Windsor also were in attendance; and when Vincent Sheean went upstairs to inform Churchill that James Thurber had just arrived, Churchill at first looked blank and then remarked, "Oh, that insane and depraved American artist." Thurber later enjoyed telling the story on himself, but at the time he was not particularly amused. After Churchill had retired for the evening, Thurber was shown a few of the great man's paintings. Unimpressed, he remarked, "The trouble with Mr. Churchill as an artist is that he is not insane and depraved enough, I guess." [22]

The Thurbers returned to Paris, made another trip to London and Scotland, then went back to France and set sail from Le Havre for home. They had been abroad nearly fourteen months, and arrived in New York on September 1, 1938, a year to the day before World War II erupted with Hitler's invasion of Poland. Soon thereafter, Thurber's beloved France would fall as well.

Many of the articles Thurber had written in Europe later were reprinted in his collection called *My World – and Welcome to It*. In a brief introduction to his pieces about France, he wrote that while "so many signs and intimations" of the looming war had been apparent to them while traveling overseas, he left it to others "better equipped" than he to write about ominous portents. He chose instead to write "of the France which so many of us will always love, the France which we know will rise again." [23]

In fact, his aversion to polemics notwithstanding, within a year of his return to the United States, Thurber would write and illustrate his own extraordinary comment on the insanity of war, *The Last Flower,* producing it at the conclusion of what may have been his most astonishing surge of creativity. Perhaps he was spurred on by a sense of impending personal catastrophe, by a wish to get as much as possible down on paper while he could still see it.

After being away for more than a year, Thurber felt slightly estranged from *The New Yorker,* and many of its regular staff members, to his mid-forties eye, looked unconscionably young. He no longer had an office at the magazine, and his visits there were infrequent. "I feel that I am looked upon as an outsider, possibly a has-been," he wrote to E. B. White. "The aging humorist I suppose is bound to be a sad figure." [24]

He and Helen moved into a rented, 225-year-old house in Woodbury, Connecticut, and he set to work on projects that would prove he was far from a has-been, aging though he was.

Thurber's father died early in 1939, and the support of his mother and brothers became entirely his responsibility. He had been their chief support for years already. His father had last held a steady job in 1931; his brother Robert, always sickly, had no success managing several bookstores Thurber financed; his brother William was also a repeated failure in business, and his mother's income from stock in the produce company founded by her father had evaporated. So increased financial responsibilities, as well as personal fears, fueled Thurber's inspiration. Casuals, cartoons, illustrations for famous poetic chestnuts, trenchant fables, and a successful Broadway play, written in collaboration with Elliott Nugent, all sprang from his brain in the next year and a half.

Of the casuals Thurber wrote during this period, "What Do You Mean It *Was* Brillig?" is one of the best-remembered, most reprinted, and most enduringly funny examples of his wordplay, even though many modern readers rightly cringe at the racial smugness behind Thurber's delight in the malapropisms of Margaret (renamed Della

71

in the story), the black woman he referred to privately as his "new cullud maid." But the servant who took great pride in her younger brother's high score on the "silver-service eliminations," who solemnly reported that delivery men had arrived with "the reeves" (the Christmas wreaths "for the windas"), who had another brother who "works into an incinerator where they burn the refuge," having done so "since the Armitage" (Armistice), and whose other language lapses would have enthralled Lewis Carroll, was not dumb. She was simply uneducated. And she also was smarter than Thurber knew. She correctly observed that his mind worked "so fast his body can't keep up with it."[25] Indeed, it couldn't.

Throughout 1939 and 1940, Thurber added new and sprightly elements to his oeuvre: fables and illustrated poems. As he later observed, concise, properly crafted fables "can say a great deal about human life," and Thurber's miniature tales pointedly touched on themes that had either long preoccupied or more recently troubled him, from female irascibility to fascism's perfidy. The fables' morals – deftly paraphrased, punned, or garbled versions of conventional, even trite axioms – add to the rich ironies in the tales, which upend traditional beliefs.[26]

In an autobiographical fable, "The Shrike and the Chipmunks," a pestering female chipmunk (not unlike Althea) hectors her artistically inclined, less practical husband. When she insists they exercise and go for a walk "in the bright sunlight," they both are attacked and killed by a shrike. The moral: "Early to rise and early to bed makes a male healthy and wealthy and dead." A parable on the rise of Nazism, "The Rabbits Who Caused All the Trouble," describes how a pack of wolves "descended on the rabbits for their own good, and imprisoned them in a dark cave, for their own protection." It ends with the moral, "Run, don't walk, to the nearest desert island." And in a twist on the tale of Little Red Riding Hood, "The Little Girl and the Wolf," the supposedly innocent tyke quickly realizes that "even in a nightcap a wolf does not look any more like your grandmother than the Metro-Goldwyn lion looks like Calvin Coolidge." Consequently, "the little girl took an automatic out of her basket and shot the wolf dead." The moral: "It is not so easy to fool little girls nowadays as it used to be."[27] The theme underlying all these fables is that the bromides of the past no longer apply. The established conservative wisdom found in the fables of Aesop or LaFontaine presupposes a world of moral certainties; Thurber's fables warn that life is unpredictable and full of unanticipated perils. In almost all of Thurber's fables, expectations are exploded, supposed truisms are twisted, and reality does battle with imagination and illusion. Thurber's hare beats the tortoise, who had believed in the outcome of the old fable. The moral: "A new broom may sweep clean, but never trust an old saw."

The best known and most beloved of all Thurber fables is "The Unicorn in the Garden," in which a typically pleasant but put-upon Thurber husband is entranced to discover a white unicorn with a golden horn quietly eating roses and lilies in his garden. Awakening his shrewish wife to inform her of this wondrous phenomenon, the man is met with an icy stare. "You are a booby," she tells him, "and I am going to have you put in the booby-hatch." She calls the police and a psychiatrist, tells them to bring a straitjacket and then – in an O. Henryish twist that was also a Thurber trademark – she is bundled off to the booby-hatch herself when her husband blandly denies having seen a unicorn in the garden. The moral: "Don't count your boobies until they are hatched." The man not only lives happily ever after, but the fable itself subsequently found its way onto the stage and was transferred to the screen as an animated cartoon. And, typically, Thurber never revealed whether the unicorn was an illusion, or actually existed, or was simply the man's clever device for disposing of his wife.[28]

The nine poems Thurber chose to illustrate – among them Whittier's "Barbara Frietchie," Longfellow's "Excelsior," and Rose Hartwick Thorpe's "Curfew Must Not Ring Tonight" – were then endemic to a basic grammar school curriculum and familiar to practically every reader who had once been forced to memorize and perhaps even recite them. The childlike quality of Thurber's illustrations was ideally suited to these hoary rhymes of childhood, which haunted the memories of so many adults. Most readers probably felt they could draw just as well as Thurber, or no worse, and perhaps believed they might have produced similar doodles to depict the action in the poems. Harold Ross, like Thurber a child of the late Victorian era, especially loved them. All of the rhymes were romantic, sentimental paeans to courage, determination, and other Victorian verities, and Thurber's effort to depict them realistically punctured the platitudes.[29] The poems and fables later were combined in one book, *Fables for Our Time and Famous Poems Illustrated.*

Of all the stories Thurber wrote that year – indeed, of all the stories he ever wrote – the best was "The Secret Life of Walter Mitty." In it he attained, as Burton Bernstein puts it, the "supreme distillation" of all his characters and themes: "the emasculated, daydreaming little man, a would-be Conradian figure hiding in a three-button suit; the emasculating, practical wife, a virago hiding inside a shrew; the love-fear of modern machinery; the attraction of fantasy as a release from reality; and, as always, the fascination for words. Here it all was, put together clearly, brilliantly, definitively."[30]

"We're going through!" The Commander's voice was like thin ice breaking. He wore his full-dress uniform, with the heavily braided white cap pulled down rakishly over one cold gray eye. "We can't make it, sir. It's spoiling for a hurricane, if you ask me." "I'm not asking you, Lieutenant Berg," said the Commander. "Throw on the power lights! Rev her up to 8,500! We're going through!" The pounding of the cylinders increased: ta-pocketa-pocketa-pocketa-*pocketa-pocketa*. The Commander stared at the ice forming on the pilot window. He walked over and twisted a row of complicated dials. "Switch on No. 8 auxiliary!" he shouted. "Switch on No. 8 auxiliary!" repeated Lieutenant Berg. "Full strength in No. 3 turret!" shouted the Commander. "Full strength in No. 3 turret!" The crew, bending to their various tasks in the huge, hurtling eight-engined Navy hydroplane, looked at each other and grinned. "The Old Man'll get us through," they said to one another. "The Old Man ain't afraid of Hell!" . . .

"Not so fast! You're driving too fast!" said Mrs. Mitty. "What are you driving so fast for?"

"Hmm?" said Walter Mitty. He looked at his wife, in the seat beside him, with shocked astonishment. She seemed grossly unfamiliar, like a strange woman who had yelled at him in a crowd. "You were up to fifty-five," she said. "You know I don't like to go more than forty. You were up to fifty-five." Walter Mitty drove on toward Waterbury in silence, the roaring of the SN202 through the worst storm in twenty years of Navy flying fading in the remote, intimate airways of his mind. "You're tensed up again," said Mrs. Mitty. "It's one of your days. I wish you'd let Dr. Renshaw look you over." [31]

Thurber liked to exaggerate the labors that went into his stories, as if the number of hours expended or words employed would somehow give weight to what the unsophisticated reader might otherwise view as a light endeavor. In fact, according to Helen, he was a fast writer who only had to rewrite certain troublesome pieces many times. [32] Thurber later would tell Alistair Cooke that he had to work "night and day" for eight weeks to compose the "4,000 words" that went into "Walter

Mitty," which he claimed to have rewritten fifteen times. In truth, the story contains just 2,500 words and probably caused him no special trouble.[33]

Its basic concept had been percolating within him ever since he wrote the high school prophecy about his daring exploits aboard the "Seairo-plane." In "Mitty" the fantasy just simply – and magically – reached its peak in a masterpiece of brief, ironic comedy. Reveling in ersatz technical terminology, the clichés of B-movie melodramas, and the conventions of pulp fiction potboilers, Mitty continues to escape the mundane demands of his nagging wife by imagining himself as a skilled surgeon capable of repairing a balky anesthetizer while performing a delicate operation for "obstreosis of the ductal tract"; an unflappable defendant on trial for murder; an Army Air Corps ace off to fly "forty kilometers through hell"; and a condemned prisoner, coolly facing a firing squad – "Walter Mitty the Undefeated, inscrutable to the last."

The impact of "Mitty" was astounding from the moment it appeared in *The New Yorker* of March 18, 1939. It has been reprinted innumerable times in textbooks and other publications, and within a few years its hero's name and the sound he attributed to every complicated machine – "ta-pocketa-pocketa" – entered the language. During World War II, "ta-pocketa-pocketa" was used on some front lines as a password, fighter pilots would identify themselves on the radio as "Walter Mitty" or "Ta-pocketa," and Walter Mitty clubs were popular among servicemen. Extravagant daydreaming has been dubbed the Walter Mitty Syndrome by the British medical magazine *The Lancet,* and laypeople as well as physicians have long since diagnosed woolgatherers of their acquaintance as Walter Mittys.[34]

The story itself has become, as Charles S. Holmes observed, "part of our modern mythology and folklore."[35] It even was adapted, unsuccessfully, as an opera, an off-Broadway musical, and an inappropriately elaborate 1947 movie musical starring Danny Kaye. Thurber later said the film should have been called "The Public Life of Danny Kaye."[36] The only remotely acceptable transformation of the piece employed the medium best suitable to imagination – radio – and starred the one performer, other than Thurber himself, best suited to the role: Robert Benchley.

Toward the end of his life, Thurber said that Mitty was based on "every other man I have ever known," although longtime family friends saw a great deal of Thurber's father and brother William in the character. Surely it is an archetype with which countless readers could – and still can – identify.* "When the story was printed in *The New Yorker*," Thurber recalled, "six men from around the country, including a Des Moines dentist, wrote and asked me how I had got to know them so well."

"No writer can ever put his finger on the exact inspiration of any character in fiction that is worthwhile, in my estimation," Thurber wrote. "Even those commonly supposed to be taken from real characters rarely show much similarity in the end."[37]

More than a smattering of similarity, however, could be found between Ohio State University and the large Midwestern college that was the setting for another of Thurber's outstanding creations during his

---

*Actor D. B. Sweeney told CNN News in 1992 that he enjoyed "the Walter Mitty experience" of skating with professional hockey players in the film *The Cutting Edge*. On the March 22, 1992, broadcast of ABC News, Forrest Sawyer introduced a story about would-be pleasure boat builders by saying, "All of us have our Walter Mitty dream worlds." And in an interview for the 1992 documentary series "The Class of the Twentieth Century," former *Washington Post* editor Benjamin Bradlee, who oversaw the paper's Pulitzer Prize-winning investigation of the Watergate scandal, said he still dreamed "in my Walter Mitty way" of interviewing Richard Nixon. Nixon himself, wrote Henry Kissinger, "lived out a Walter Mitty dream of toughness that did not come naturally."

banner year 1939, the play on which he and Elliott Nugent collaborated, *The Male Animal*. Its success made Thurber financially independent at last, free to do whatever he wished. His worsening eye trouble would, for a time, make that a hollow triumph.

During their student days, Thurber and Nugent had promised each other that they would collaborate on something, sometime. By now Nugent was a well-established actor and director in Hollywood, and at first he was uninterested in Thurber's idea for a comedy about the rivalry between an academic and an erstwhile football hero over the scholarly man's attractive wife. But Thurber persisted and Nugent eventually realized that the slim storyline could be enhanced by appending to the plot a plea for academic freedom. He agreed to undertake the project and came east for an initial brainstorming session at the Algonquin Hotel in January 1939. Other commitments then intervened, but in June the Thurbers gave up their rented Connecticut house, put their trusty Ford aboard a ship and took a long, wiltingly hot voyage via Havana and the Panama Canal to Nugent's home in Los Angeles.[38]

The intense, unrelenting sun on the way to California had bothered Thurber's eye terribly and brought on another episode of temporary blindness. Even when his vision returned, his ability to see was further diminished. His collaboration with Nugent proved stormy. Thurber loved the theater but was out of his element when it came to the requirements of dramatic structure. "It is very hard for a man who has always just sort of started to write pieces and begun to make scrawls on paper, wondering what they were going to turn into, to encounter what is known as the three-act play," he later wrote. "The three-act play has sharp, concrete edges, rigid spacings, a complete dependence on time and more than a hundred rules, all basic. 'You can't run a first act fifty minutes'; 'you can't have people just sitting and talking'; 'you can't play comedy in a dim light'." He would never work well within these and other dramatic constraints, and his subsequent efforts at writing plays were for naught.[39]

Thurber also found Hollywood distasteful. It had attractions – primarily nocturnal drinking bouts at Chasen's restaurant with such buddies as Humphrey Bogart, James Cagney, Nunnally Johnson, and a newcomer named Ronald Reagan – and he was feted at innumerable parties. Although he had long been a movie fan, Thurber generally disliked motion picture people, particularly the unlettered, apparently uncouth moguls who were, in many prominent instances, Jewish. Ironically, when he wrote a scathing send-up of the supposedly typical Jewish movie producer, "The Man Who Hated Moonbaum," in which one Jewish movie producer voices loathing for another Jewish movie producer, the person whose inanities he reproduced almost verbatim was Leo McCarey, as Irish as the Blarney Stone.[40]

Whatever anti-Semitism Thurber may have harbored appears to have been exorcised by the Holocaust. After World War II, he refused to associate with one Connecticut neighbor because the man was openly anti-Semitic, and once he picked up a chair and smashed it to pieces when another wealthy, right-wing neighbor averred that some of his best friends were Jewish. Mark Van Doren, who witnessed this episode, believed Thurber despised the cliché as much as the smarmy sentiment.[41]

Over a four-month period, Thurber and Nugent alternately developed the characters, scenes, and dialogue that told the story of Tommy Turner, an idealistic English professor who is at odds with a former football hero, Joe Ferguson, over the affections of Turner's wife, Ellen. At the same time, Turner also is battling a boorish university trustee, Ed Keller, over the right to read to his composition class the then-well-known open letter that anarchist Bartolomeo Vanzetti wrote just prior to his execution in 1927. It is a play that still is being performed by summer stock troupes today as a period piece, but it carried considerable impact just prior to World War II and even more when it was revived on Broadway in the early 1950s, during the McCarthy period.

By the late summer of 1939, *The Male Animal* was well enough along to allow Thurber and Helen to put their car on a train and head back east. His funds were running low, as were his spirits. The outbreak of World War II that September depressed him. Again settled in the Algonquin Hotel with Helen, he spent just one evening after dinner writing and drawing what may be the most touching work he ever created, *The Last Flower.*[42]

This exquisitely written, audaciously simple parable describes the globe's recovery from the destruction of World War XII, beginning with the only flower to survive it, and the inexorable slide of a revived mankind into World War XIII, which ends in a chillingly prophetic, nuclearlike annihilation that leaves alive only one man, one woman, and one flower. Somehow it is a curiously hopeful tale, and, given the grim subject, gently amusing. How else can one react except with a grin to a plague of large rabbits, or preening militarists, or moping but wise dogs abandoning their fallen masters? And knowing that the resurrection of civilization was begun by nurturing a single flower, how else can one view the story's ending except optimistically? Thurber quickly polished the text, inked in his pencil sketches, dedicated the book to his daughter, Rosemary, "in the wistful hope that her world will be better than mine," and gave it to Harper & Row for prompt publication. It came out in time for Christmas, 1939.

W. H. Auden, among other reviewers, was lavish with his praise. While quibbling that *The Last Flower* was "at once too pessimistic and not pessimistic enough," Auden nevertheless wrote that "it would be as impertinent as it is unnecessary to praise Mr. Thurber's work; everyone knows and loves it."[43] Catherine McGehee Kenney calls *The Last*

Flower "the verbal/visual equivalent of a finely executed concerto: the boy, the girl, and the flower are the soloists of hope, life, and love against the orchestrated background of hate, despair, and destruction."[44]

Having completed *The Last Flower,* Thurber boarded a westbound train with Helen to return to California and the initial tryout performances of *The Male Animal.* It opened on October 16, 1939, in San Diego and later moved to Santa Barbara and Los Angeles for additional preliminary performances, playing before audiences filled with such celebrities as Walt Disney, Myrna Loy, Harold Lloyd, director King Vidor, and Groucho Marx, who offered what Thurber considered the best advice: trim the jokes and emphasize the serious theme. Thurber, always a frustrated thespian, was delighted to be involved in a theatrical production, but the maddening rewrites, contradictory advice, and creative tensions drove him batty. "God knows you get all kinds of viewpoints," he later wrote to E. B. White. "Everybody wants to change this or that or put in business or suggest lines. When I got out there the play had lines in it and business suggested by secretaries, cousins, mothers, bat boys, doormen, and little old women in shawls."[45] Thurber's relationship with Nugent was badly strained, and when the play closed after a week in Los Angeles, it appeared unlikely they would ever get it to Broadway.

Nevertheless, Nugent followed Thurber back to New York and they put in another ten days rewriting the script. They presented it to a prominent producer, Herman Shumlin, who astonished them by immediately agreeing to put it on and direct it himself. Tryouts and rewrites in Princeton and Baltimore, where Thurber got to meet his longtime hero, H. L. Mencken, preceded the play's Broadway opening on January 9, 1940. It starred Nugent as Tommy Turner, Leon Ames as Joe Ferguson, Ruth Matteson as Turner's wife, Ellen (replacing Mary Astor, who had originated the role in California), and a largely un-

known but beautiful young actress named Gene Tierney in an inge-
nue part.

The opening night audience greeted the final curtain with cries for
the author, which Thurber was more than delighted to answer with
bows and a curtain speech. Enthusiastic reviews by the critics, who
likened it to *Life with Father* and *The Man Who Came to Dinner,* the
season's other comedy triumphs, assured *The Male Animal* a long and
prosperous run. After the play's success, Thurber had Broadway in his
pocket and loved every minute of it.[46]

Success proved as perilous as failure might have been. The hectic
weeks leading up to the Broadway opening were followed by days just as
hectic, and long, drink-filled nights. The rounds of interviews, parties,
and attendant hoopla took a physical toll on both Thurber and Helen,
leading to an almost simultaneous collapse: she ended up in the hospital, suffering from anemia; he found himself "down in bed in the hotel,
running a fever, seeing mice with boxing gloves on, and the like," he
wrote to friends.[47] More ominously, he suffered another bout of serious eye trouble, and his ophthalmologist, Dr. Bruce, decided that the
cataract surgery could not be postponed any longer. A date was set for
an operation in June.

Earlier, in 1939, Thurber had written to Dr. Bruce that he did not
want to "go through life like a blindfolded man looking for a black
sock on a black carpet. . . . Life is no good to me at all unless I can read,
type and draw. I would sell out for 13 cents."[48] Now at the height of his
powers, he realized that blindness could soon be his lot.

Writing by Ear

To rest and prepare for the impending eye surgery, which his ophthalmologist now concluded would require separate operations in June and October, Thurber and Helen retreated to Bermuda. He still could see well enough on occasion to read, but the opacities in his eye caused by the cataract largely obscured his sight and left him frustrated. He likened his visual obstruction to "spaniel hair," and wrote in a grim but vaguely hopeful mood to Dr. Bruce: "I probably see as well as the water buffalo, reputedly the blindest of all large jungle animals. It is interesting to note that the water buffalo can lick a tiger in spite of his opacities and indifferent, if not, indeed, detached retina."

"There are more things in my eye than were dreamed of in Horatio's day, anyway, or maybe Hamlet had opacities and thought they were ghosts. This would also explain Macbeth's looking at nothing at all in the banquet scene and shouting, 'Take any other form than that!' I think I know how he felt, if it was opacities he saw and not Banquo."[1]

The Thurbers returned to Connecticut in June, and he entered the Columbia Presbyterian Medical Center's Institute of Ophthalmology for the first round of surgery. Dr. Bruce removed the cataract, and for a brief period Thurber's vision improved. Then it clouded up again, although in August he still was capable of using his hunt-and-peck technique on a typewriter to compose a rollicking and affectionate baseball story, "You Could Look It Up," full of malapropisms and grammatical gaffes in the Ring Lardner manner. This tale of how the desperate manager of a foundering, turn-of-the-century pennant contender hires a midget to pinch-hit and draw a crucial walk, published in *The Saturday Evening Post* in 1941, was the inspiration for Bill Veeck's memorable stunt a decade later, when he put three-foot, seven-inch Eddie Gaedel in to bat for the dismal St. Louis Browns. (Veeck readily doffed his cap to Thurber in an interview with *The Sporting News*.) In real life, Gaedel dutifully followed instructions and drew his walk; in Thurber's story, the midget, gloriously monickered Pearl du Monville, ignores directions, hits a pitch, is tossed out at first and then grabbed by the infuriated manager and thrown sky-high. The heroic center fielder of the opposing team manages to save the midget's life by catching him before he hits the ground and "bust to pieces like a dollar watch on a asphalt street." [2]

Despite the grand humor and high spirits in "You Could Look It Up," Thurber was growing increasingly pessimistic about his ability to continue writing and drawing as he awaited his next session on the surgeon's table in October. He therefore was grateful when his old *New Yorker* colleague Ralph Ingersoll, now the editor of the liberal, advertisement-free New York tabloid *PM*, offered him the opportunity to write a twice-weekly newspaper column on any subject he wished for $100 a piece. [3] The columns and spot drawings he did between September 1940 and July 1941 under the heading "If You Ask Me" were in many ways descendants of his old "Credos and Curios" pieces for the Columbus *Dispatch,* albeit far better written. In one column, Thurber sought to deflate the smug American assumption that foreign wiles were no match for Yankee horse sense. He retrieved from obscurity a long-forgotten minor work by Will Rogers, *Letters of a Self-Made Diplomat to His President,* published in 1926, to show that the legendary insight and caginess of the cowboy philosopher/comedian completely failed him following an encounter with Benito Mussolini. Rogers had informed President Coolidge and the public that Mussolini was perhaps not as great a man as Theodore Roosevelt, but was "a kind of cross between Roosevelt, Red Grange, Babe Ruth when the Babe is really good, the older LaFollette, a touch of Borah, Bryan of '96, Samuel Gompers, and Tunney." Instead of being as shrewd an observer of foreign politicians as he supposedly was of domestic ones, Rogers really was an international naif, as were many Americans. "This grinning Yankee at Victor Emmanuel's court was bound to make a fool of himself," Thurber concluded.[4]

Most of Thurber's *PM* pieces were far less substantial, but lightweight though they may have been, the columns gave him a not-too-taxing chance to keep his hand in writing and maintain a sense of productivity in the shadow of the scalpel.

Thurber's second eye operation — there would be five of them over eleven months — was performed on October 22, 1940, after 1:30 P.M., the time of day having been set as an accommodation to Thurber's increasingly daffy mother. She believed in astrology and had implored Dr. Bruce to schedule the operation according to Thurber's "planets." In a subsequent, slightly pathetic letter, Mame Thurber even offered to give Dr. Bruce one of her own eyes as a substitute for her son's.[5]

The second operation, for glaucoma and iritis, was not successful. Like all of the eye surgery Thurber underwent, it was performed under local, not general, anesthetic, and he endured considerable postoperative pain. He had to remain hospitalized for thirty-one days, an incarceration that shattered his nerves. He suffered a breakdown, a deep, debilitating depression that lasted six months and which he overcame only by sheer intestinal fortitude. "They dragged old Jamie through all the corridors of hell, where I left most of my weight and two thirds of my nerves," he wrote in a May 1941 letter to his friends the Williamses in Bermuda, "but things have quieted down now." [6]

The quiet did not last for long. Moving up to Martha's Vineyard for the summer, Thurber developed a new, painfully slow method of composition by which he began writing again. The results were striking, and in some ways bizarre. He used a pencil to scrawl words he could no longer see on page after page of yellow paper. Where once he had possessed a tight, neat handwriting, he now produced large, unevenly spaced letters and words, only a few to a page. Helen typed up the scraggly manuscript, which Thurber would listen to and then revise in his head, employing the astounding memory of which he had always been proud.[7] In this manner he briefly continued his *PM* columns and retreated to the world of childhood fantasy, starting the draft of a children's book which became an enchanting fairy tale, *Many Moons*. He also wrote what Helen would later call his "horror stories," two pieces that foreshadowed further emotional upheaval: "The Whip-Poor-Will" and "A Friend to Alexander." Both are stories of men gone mad.[8]

In "The Whip-Poor-Will," an already delusional, nightmare-ridden man named Kinstrey is driven berserk by the incessant chirping of a nearby whippoorwill, a harbinger of death, the hired cook says. Kinstrey's mind snaps and he kills his servants, his wife, and then himself with a long carving knife, hoarsely wondering aloud before the carnage commences, "Who do you do first?" In "A Friend to Alexander," a man named Andrews, obsessed by dreams of a smug Aaron Burr and a doomed Alexander Hamilton, begins practicing with a pistol in order to fight a duel with Burr's ghost to avenge Hamilton's death. Andrews dies of a heart attack while asleep, his right hand frozen "as if gripping the handle of a pistol." [9]

A third short story Thurber wrote that summer, "The Cane in the

Corridor," deals with the revenge a recently hospitalized man seeks to inflict on a friend who failed to visit him. It reverberates with Thurber's own fury over the failure of Wolcott Gibbs to call on him throughout his hospitalization for eye surgery.[10]

Some of Thurber's friends were disturbed by the dark twist some of his stories had taken – and, as it turned out, with reason. After finishing the first draft of *Many Moons* with a flourish, he suddenly "went into a tailspin, crashed, and burst into flames," as he later described his second breakdown in a letter to Dr. Bruce.[11] Another bout of iritis, heavy drinking, and terror at the thought that along with his sight he was losing his power to write as well as draw led to his irrational insistence that he could no longer stand to be alone with Helen. He demanded that they move into the nearby house of their friends John (Jap) Gude and his wife, Liz. There Thurber sat silent and brooding in the living room, staring into empty space, occasionally hallucinating. At one point he grabbed Gude tightly by the arm and pleaded, "Promise me you won't let them put me away." The Gudes wisely contacted Dr. Ruth Fox, who had experience dealing with alcoholics, and she treated Thurber with massive injections of vitamin B-1, which had the odd side-effect of turning a forelock of his now-white hair jet black. His recovery was slow but steady. "The things that inhabit the woods I fell into are not nice," he wrote to Dr. Bruce that August. "I never want to crash there again if I can help it."[12]

When Thurber returned to New York in the fall, he went to see a psychiatrist, Dr. Marian Kenworthy, whose assessment heartened him. She told Helen: "Your husband no more needs psychiatric treatment than my dog does."[13] The fact that Thurber put such trust in two female physicians, Doctors Fox and Kenworthy, prompted him to insist years later that his "reputation as a woman-hating writer is largely myth and misconception. . . . Women psychiatrists try to find out what is the matter with you, but the male ones love to show off their implementation and try out their nomenclature on you." [14]

Thurber's recovery, however, took a long time. During that summer of 1941, as he began fighting his way out of what he called "the bowels of terror," he met critic and poet Mark Van Doren on the Vineyard. One afternoon while chatting on the lawn of Van Doren's home, Thurber began to weep. He asked Van Doren if blindness might be a punishment for the type of writing he had done — making fun of people, highlighting their weaknesses, not celebrating their strengths. Van Doren, a great admirer of Thurber's unique gifts as a writer, assured him that humorists have an important role to play in pointing out the absence of goodness and intelligence in the world. Thurber was consoled; but the doubts he expressed about the value of his work, his fear that it was seen as trivial and not properly appreciated, would plague him for the rest of his life. [15]

Thurber had periodic mental relapses, as well as what he later called a castration complex. [16] He feared that his virility had been irrevocably sapped by his eye operations and subsequent setbacks, so he sought to prove his potency by trying to make love to Helen constantly while they were on Martha's Vineyard. Upon their return to New York, Thurber directed his attentions elsewhere. He purportedly became involved with a secretary at *The New Yorker* but required the guiding arm of an office boy to visit her apartment clandestinely. That office boy was a diminutive, mischievous teenager named Truman Capote. Once, while helping Thurber to dress following a tryst, Capote, then eighteen, apparently put Thurber's socks on inside out, alerting Helen to the fact that something was amiss. According to Capote, an infuriated Thurber accused Capote of having done it on purpose, but for some reason he continued to use him as an escort to the secretary's flat. [17]

During the winter, Thurber wrote a pleasant but slight piece recalling an unimaginative high school English teacher under whose numbing tutelage he had suffered, and another casual article about one of his quirky ancestors. He also wrote a brutal review of John Steinbeck's novel *The Moon Is Down* for *The New Republic,* lambasting Steinbeck's unrealistic portrayal of warfare and apparent lack of outrage over the Nazi invasion of Norway. When Steinbeck's editor complained to *The New Republic* that Thurber's review had been a "slap in the face" to Steinbeck, Thurber replied, "I am sorry about that slap in the face. I didn't realize my hand was open." He was a tough, perceptive literary critic.[18]

There were diversions besides the *New Yorker* secretary that dismal winter. Thurber and Helen returned to Columbus in March 1942 to participate in the world premiere of the Warner Bros. movie version of *The Male Animal,* which had been directed by Elliott Nugent and starred Henry Fonda, Olivia de Havilland, and Jack Carson. The hoopla included a Male Animal Ball with Cab Calloway's Orchestra, a luncheon at the Ohio State Faculty Club, a huge dinner at Thurber's old O.S.U. fraternity house, and a sentimental visit to the *Dispatch* newspaper office, all leading up to the movie's debut, at which Thurber's mother and brothers also were in attendance. The film was a critical success, but the whole event had been exhausting and the Thurbers were glad to return to New York.[* 19]

In the spring of 1942 they rented a house in Cornwall, Connecticut, and found the town and its surroundings so congenial that they decided to settle there. Mark Van Doren and his wife, Dorothy, lived nearby, and the Thurbers soon became close friends with others in the area,

---

*In 1951, Warner's did a terrible musical version of the play, *She's Working Her Way Through College,* which was one more nail in the coffin of Ronald Reagan's movie career.

including Rose Algrant, a prep school French teacher whose charming personality and wonderful Franco-Turkish accent and English mala-propisms delighted Thurber.

The restorative powers of Cornwall that summer led to the compo-sition of one of Thurber's finest short stories, "The Catbird Seat," the hero of which is a meek, Mittylike filing clerk named Erwin Martin. He devises an ingenious, bloodless way to "rub out" Mrs. Ulgine Barrows, the domineering, insufferable special assistant to Mr. Fitweiler, presi-dent of F&S, the firm where Martin works. Certain that Mrs. Barrows is about to wreak havoc on his beloved filing system, the nonsmoking, teetotaling Martin visits her apartment, lights up a Camel, downs a Scotch-and-soda, and instead of murdering her outright, as he origi-nally planned, decides to do her in by way of deception. He tells her that he's a heroin addict, plans to murder Fitweiler, and will be "coked to the gills" when he does it. The next day Mrs. Barrows reports Martin to Mr. Fitweiler, and when Martin, the soul of probity, plausibly denies her accusations, she is hauled away screaming, not unlike the wife of the man who saw the unicorn in the garden.[20]

With "The Catbird Seat," as perfectly polished a gem as any he ever wrote, Thurber seemed on his way to recovery. He and Helen also com-piled a new collection of previously published pieces, including "The Secret Life of Walter Mitty," and brought it out under the title *My World – and Welcome to It* in October 1942.*

The volume was enthusiastically received both here and in blitz-battered Britain, giving Thurber a sense that he was somehow contrib-uting to the war effort by lightening many dark days. More than twenty years later, John Mortimer, the British barrister best known today as the

---

*The title was used for a short-lived NBC television situation comedy, loosely based on Thurber's mordant view of life. It lasted only one season, 1969–70.[21]

Charles and Mame (Fisher)
Thurber with Robert (in pram),
William, and James.

The three
Thurber brothers
(Jamie is at left).

Thurber as a high
school student.

Thurber on the
threshold of fame.

Jim, Althea, and
Rosemary Thurber
at Sandy Hook,
New Jersey, 1932.

Helen and James
Thurber, mid-1930s.

Mark Van Doren,
Thurber, and E. B. White
(Condax Studios, 1953).

Head table at Rosemary
Thurber's wedding
(Condax Studios, 1953).
E. B. White sits between
Thurber and Althea;
Helen partly hidden
by Thurber.

James Thurber in Bermuda, 1930s.

creator of *Rumpole of the Bailey,* wrote that it was impossible in war-time England to find a home without a Thurber book, "dog-eared from fire-watching, bent from the gas-mask case." Thurber still remained "part of the standard equipment of the British Intellectual" two decades after the war, Mortimer wrote.[22] Toward the end of World War II, Franklin Roosevelt sent word that he wanted Thurber to draw the cover of a small, privately printed pamphlet of bogus recipes entitled *Thirty-four Ways to Cook Brussels Sprouts.* FDR was having the booklet made up to perpetuate a practical joke he was playing on Winston Churchill. He had told Churchill's wife, Clementine, that Brussels sprouts were the favorite vegetable in America, and he wanted a Thurber drawing of famished Yanks lining up to attack a huge bowl of them. Thurber dutifully and with some difficulty did the drawing but never got a copy of the booklet, which miffed him. Presumably its cover did not impress Churchill.[23]

An inability to get strictly rationed fuel oil for their rented house in Cornwall compelled the Thurbers to move back into Manhattan in January 1943. Thurber felt ready to begin making the rounds of his favorite pubs again, and with the brightest day being indistinguishable to him now from the darkest night, he cared little for the hours he kept.

Early in 1943, Thurber learned about the Zeiss loop, a magnifying device worn by defense workers laboring on delicate, precision equipment. By using one, he found that he was able to see figures well enough to draw cartoons on twenty-four-inch by sixteen-inch paper under a bright light. For all of his continuing disparagement of his artistic abilities, he desperately wanted to draw again. Wearing a Zeiss loop helmet made him look "like a welder from Mars," he wrote to a friend, but it enabled him once again to give the world his lumpy men, women, and dogs. That list of characters would become the title of a collection of his cartoons. *Men, Women and Dogs,* published that fall, was his first such anthology of drawings in a decade, and he dedicated it to E. B. White. Although privately an agnostic, Thurber told *Newsweek,* "There must be an amiable God who had it in mind for me to do these drawings and is not opposed to them."[24]

The theatrical bug, never entirely out of Thurber's system, also recurred in 1943. He began drafting a play based on the inimitable Ross and life at *The New Yorker.* He got enough down on paper to warrant, so he thought, an announcement in *Variety* that it would be produced in November of that year. But it did not open then or ever. He would revise and tinker with it repeatedly for the rest of his life, but he was never able to put it into producible shape. His *New Yorker* memories ultimately would find their way into a book that received far more attention than any theatrical flop.

The rousing reception that greeted *Men, Women and Dogs* in late 1943 was accompanied by a series of critical hosannas for his children's book *Many Moons,* the draft of which Thurber had unintentionally left behind in the Martha's Vineyard home of the Gudes when he had suffered his breakdown there in the summer of 1941. It was discovered the following spring by the house's caretaker, and Thurber readied it for publication in the fall of 1943, with illustrations by Louis Slobodkin. The tale of a sickly little princess who will recover only if she is given the moon, it won plaudits from many, including the American Library Association, which awarded it a prize as the best picture book of the year. In the tale, the Princess Lenore is ill "from a surfeit of raspberry tarts." When she says she will get better if she is given the moon, the King's Lord High Chamberlain, Wizard, and Royal Mathematician all calculate the moon's size, content, and distance differently, but all agree it is too big and far away to obtain. The Jester, however, says that it is necessary to determine how big and far away the moon is in the Princess Lenore's opinion, and when she says it is no bigger than her thumbnail, not as high as the tree outside her window, and made of gold, the Jester has the Royal Goldsmith make a small moon for the Princess and she gets well. She is unconcerned when the moon next rises, likening its appearance in the sky to a new tooth replacing one that is lost.

Many Moons remains a popular children's classic today and was re-issued in 1990 with new illustrations by Thurber's old neighbor and friend Marc Simont.

Although Thurber had a well-deserved reputation for irascibility — Helen called his fits of melancholy, fury, and meanness "the Thurbs" — he also could be remarkably generous with encouragement, advice, and financial assistance.[25] He sent regular checks to his mother and brothers, wrote gracious introductions for the books of some friends, promoted the efforts of others, and particularly delighted in persuading Harold Ross to hire Peter De Vries, then the editor of *Poetry* magazine, as a contract writer for *The New Yorker*.

Thurber had met De Vries following publication of a graceful and keen analysis of Thurber's work that the young editor had written for *Poetry* and titled "James Thurber: The Comic Prufrock." De Vries observed that Thurber's stories, especially those in which mispronuncia-tions and word games play a central role, signaled his greater kinship with modern poets than humorists. T. S. Eliot's J. Alfred Prufrock, "lost in the fumes of introspection," De Vries wrote, is the solemn counter-part of Thurber's preoccupied, bumbling middle-aged man on the flying trapeze.[26] De Vries was not the first critic to take Thurber seriously, but few if any had done so before with such verve and wit. Their friendship was instantaneous and deepened over the years, and Thurber did *The New Yorker* special service by recruiting De Vries for its staff.

The warm reception accorded *Many Moons* encouraged Thurber to set to work on another fairy tale. He enjoyed the genre, having been a fan since childhood of L. Frank Baum's Oz books, which he termed

American-style "fairy tales with a difference." Baum, he noted in an appreciative essay, wrote in the foreword to *The Wizard of Oz* that he had endeavored to devise a story devoid of "the heartaches and nightmares" found in old European fairy tales. Thurber, for one, was glad he had failed in that supposedly noble ambition. "Children love a lot of nightmare and at least a little heartache in their books," Thurber observed.[27] And in his next fairy tale, *The Great Quillow,* he was happy to supply a bit of both. The book, illustrated by Doris Lee and published in 1944, tells of how a Thurberish toymaker named Quillow uses his wits to destroy a brutal, grasping giant named Hunder. As in the case with *Many Moons,* it remains popular and a newly illustrated edition is scheduled for publication in 1994.

Thurber might slay giants in children's books, but illness proved a more persistent, formidable foe. Late in 1944, he twice contracted lobar pneumonia, and while on a recuperative trip to Hot Springs, Virginia, that November, he suffered a burst appendix and a bout of peritonitis that nearly did him in. Somehow he – and his sense of humor – prevailed. When he was told that the surgeon who removed his appendix found it far behind his cecum, he liked to tell friends he had been the proud owner of a "hide and cecum appendix."[28]

Thurber had always been preoccupied with his age and supposed frailty, fretting about his lack of advancement in his twenties, the horrors of middle age while still in his thirties, and his status as "an aging humorist" and "has-been" in his forties. Now that he had survived serious illnesses, blindness, and a mental breakdown, he enjoyed boasting about his stamina and toughness.* He was able to return to New York shortly after his fiftieth birthday, convinced that a bright future awaited

*In an interview in August 1961, just four months before he died, Thurber boasted, "I'm sixty-six now, going on fifty, and I expect to live and work for another thirty years."[29]

him. "I have just begun to write," he advised some friends in a letter. "These are the best years. I spit on the grave of my awful forties." [30]

Indeed, his most popular collection of articles and drawings, *The Thurber Carnival,* would be published in 1945 to virtually unanimous critical acclaim and mammoth sales that kept it on the best-seller lists for nearly a year. Containing highlights from his books published over the preceding fifteen years, as well as newer pieces, it was – and remains – a stunning display of his scope and skill. It sold well over 400,000 copies that first year, and still sells today. Reviewers realized, some with a touch of surprise, that this collection of Thurber's finest works demonstrated convincingly that he was more than just an amusing staff writer for *The New Yorker,* he was a significant literary figure. "The man, or at least his work, is here to stay," observed *The New York Times.* "We can no longer be content simply to laugh at what he produces; we must make a determined effort to understand him as man and artist." [31]

Harper and Brothers, the publisher of *The Thurber Carnival,* originally had proposed entitling it *A Thurber Sampler.* Thurber ridiculed that name, telling E. B. White that it represented everything that was stuffy, old-fashioned, and commercially inept about the publisher. He could imagine the editors sipping Madeira and winding their antique pocket watches with tiny keys while they came up with it, he wrote.[32] Instead, when Thurber chose the word *carnival* for the book's title, he adopted "an apt metaphor" for his work, Catherine McGehee Kenney has written, "for like a carnival, his world is filled with games of chance, distorted mirrors, unusual animals, exhilarating and yet frightening rides through the imagination, and occasional glances at the beautiful carousel – a quieter and gentler image of harmonious movement." [33]

Thurber now found himself being likened routinely to Mark Twain. He told an interviewer, with an appropriately modest touch of skepticism: "If a humorist sells 20,000 copies, he's compared to Artemus Ward. When you sell 30,000, it's Edward Lear. Get to 60 or 70 and you're another Lewis Carroll. But at 200 to 300,000 – boy, you just gotta be Mark Twain."[34]

Income from the *Carnival* enabled Thurber to become a man of property in Twain's own adopted state, Connecticut, where he and Helen at last gave up renting residences and purchased a home of their own. The Great Good Place, as Thurber called it, echoing Henry James, was a fourteen-room colonial mansion in West Cornwall, set on a hill amid cathedral pines, overlooking a splendid valley.[35] Settled nearby were some of his closest friends – the Van Dorens, William Shirer, returned from overseas after years of international upheaval and war, of which he had been, and would be, a master chronicler, Rose Algrant, and others. Thurber became the acknowledged head of their small literary and artistic group, beloved and relished when he was kind, entertaining, and jovial; indulged, tolerated, and repeatedly forgiven when he was drunk and combative. Many evenings that ended in Thurber belittling and attacking his companions were followed by his abject apologies the next morning.

Morose and often mean-spirited when he was not working, Thurber promptly sought to follow up the *Carnival*'s success with others. Another project he brought to wonderful completion in 1945 was *The White Deer,* his personal favorite among his fairy tales. A fantasy given a medieval tone with rhythmic, alliterative prose and verse, it also is full of backward spellings, puns, anagrams, and hidden in-jokes. It even contains allusions to his visual impairment. Tocko, the one-time Royal Astronomer now reduced by fading eyesight to the role of sundial maker, engraves glum sayings on his handiworks: "After this brief light, the unending dark," and "This little light and then the night." A fearsome Black Knight who turns out to be a tiny old man in a large suit of armor observes, "When all is dark within the house, / Who knows the monster from the mouse?" [36] Thurber considered *The White Deer*, the story of the quest by three sons of a blustery, Harold Ross-like monarch for the hand of a magical maiden transformed from a fawn, to be a book for adults as well as children. Writing it, Thurber told friends, was the "most fun I ever had," and he was angered by those who saw it only as a children's story. Its critical success, however, was overwhelming, as were its sales, giving him a second best-seller to match the *Carnival*. [37]

Adorned with the Zeiss loop helmet, Thurber returned to his now appropriately enlarged drawing board and produced forty-five illustrations for *The White Deer*, as well as cartoons for two new pieces for *The New Yorker*. One, "Our New Natural History," employed winsomely extravagant puns and clichés as captions for fantastic, unknown species of Thurber's creation, such as the Hopeless Quandary, the Bodkin and the Chintz, a pair of Martinets, the Blind Rage, a Garble with an Utter in its Claws, and the Goad. The Thurberish flora thus depicted included Baker's Dozen, Shepherd's Pie, Sailor's Hornpipe, Quench, and Arpeggio. Sometimes flora and fauna were shown together, such as the Hoodwink sitting on a spray of Ragamuffin, or the Gloat near a patch of I-Told-You-So. Although his line was shaky (it had never been that steady anyhow), his invention and charm were as good as ever, if not better. Words, his growing preoccupation, were transformed into living things, the inhabitants of a special universe all his own. [38] A second new series of cartoons, "The Olden Time," put Thurber's men and women in the Middle Ages. A female-headed dragon was shown glowering at a timid knight, a man and woman were seen going face-to-face in a joust, and other vignettes of that distant, often myth-encased epoch were given the unique Thurber touch. [39]

While he was at work on these projects, Thurber also was ensnarled in a lengthy pastiche *cum* tribute to Henry James, "The Beast in the

Dingle," on which he labored sporadically for three years, ridding himself in the process of the infatuation he long had harbored for the exquisite Master of refined sensibilities. A few years later, he wrote to a fan that "the influence I had to fight off in writing was Henry James, and the influence that helped me most was that of E. B. White."[40]

Thurber's relationship with his daughter deepened during the immediate postwar years, when Rosemary, now a teenager, would spend summers at his West Cornwall home. During the rest of the year she lived with Althea (who had been remarried twice) in Amherst, Massachusetts, and attended the Northampton School for Girls. Amazingly, Rosemary was eight years old before Althea had told her that Thurber was her father. "I didn't know who this person was . . . , this tall guy who used to come and visit," she recalls.[41] Now at his Connecticut home, Rosemary enjoyed a surprisingly adult association with her father and his circle of friends, who welcomed her teenage chums almost as equals and invited them to join in their cocktail parties and other social gatherings.

Thurber took a fond but not overly intrusive interest in Rosemary's education, writing letters to the headmistress of her school in which he ruminated on educational trends, the intellectual interests (or lack of them) in youngsters, the preoccupations of youth, and what he felt were the unsettling, depressing, fearful changes in the postwar world. "In my day, when I was Rosemary's age, the greatest threat to the world was Halley's comet," he wrote. In one letter, he listed twenty books he said had influenced him and were important for any teenager's education, among them Sinclair Lewis's *Babbit,* Fitzgerald's *The Great Gatsby,* Hemingway's *The Sun Also Rises,* Clarence Day's *God and My Father,* Willa Cather's *My Mortal Enemy,* Rebecca West's *The Return of the Soldier,* E. B. White's *One Man's Meat,* Ring Lardner's *How to Write*

Short Stories, and Henry James's *Daisy Miller.* To his credit, Thurber insisted that he did not demand that Rosemary read these books. "I am a rabid antagonist of the 'Silas Marner' kind of required reading," he wrote to the headmistress. Only the good books he discovered on his own "stirred my interest as a writer," he contended.[42]

He came to terms, if not peace, with his near-total blindness. He wrote to Dr. Bruce, now back from the war with a combat-induced hearing impairment, that he knew it would "be harder to get an instrument in my eye again than to find you for the next war." He was, Thurber wrote, "perfectly satisfied to let well enough alone," adding a humorous hope that Bruce's "ears have somehow turned the corner and that you will eventually be able to hear what people are whispering about you." But he ended the letter with a grimly jocular: "I'll be seeing you one of these days. Yours, Jim the blind humorist ha, ha T."[43]

The Zeiss loop, large yellow paper and black chalk, a specially lighted drawing board custom-made for him by General Electric, a mechanical pencil from Czechoslovakia that made a line that glowed like neon – all were employed in his efforts to keep on drawing. He still made light of his artistic creations, writing to a woman who claimed that her youngster's scrawls equaled his own: "Your son can certainly draw as well as I can. The only trouble is he hasn't been through as much."[44] Eventually, however, he decided that the toil required to continue drawing was too much. The last original cartoon he did for *The New Yorker* appeared on November 1, 1947. It was a simple spot of two boxers and carried no caption. His final original drawing for publication was an apt self-portrait with dogs, which he scratched out on black paper with white chalk for the July 9, 1951, issue of *Time.* It was printed on the cover to accompany a glowing profile of him. With that, Thurber's drawing came to an end, although he sometimes used one of his long, slim fingers to outline a Thurber dog in the air, and once even did so with a small flashlight to accommodate a magazine photographer, who used a prolonged exposure to capture the fleeting image.[45]

By now Thurber had perfected his method for writing stories in his head. His wife and friends came to recognize a certain look of preoccupation that came over him as he toyed with words, phrases, sentences, and paragraphs in his mind; he seemed at times to be working constantly, even during meals and at parties. "Stop writing, Thurber!" Helen might snap if she realized he was ignoring guests – or her. His powers of concentration proved as phenomenal as his memory. He could retain the minutest details of texts that were read to him and conjure them up at the appropriate point when composing a factual piece. Once he had a draft completed, he would dictate it to a secretary; when it was typed, they would go over it and he would recast a sentence here, change a word there, and revise the work repeatedly until it sounded right to him.

Letters were written the same way, and he maintained a voluminous correspondence, answering thousands of letters from strangers as well as friends. Toward the end of his life, Thurber would tell interviewers that it had taken him ten years to perfect his technique for "ear writing," yet no matter how adept he became at it, something was always missing. Occasionally he still would try to write with a pencil. Helen would see him sitting in his study, making meaningless scrawls on copy paper. The urge to engage in the physical act of writing never left him.[46]

What Thurber was writing were some first-rate short pieces, as good as any he produced before World War II. During 1948 and 1949, he wrote about one casual a month. Among them were "File and Forget," a fictional, amusingly infuriating correspondence between an author named J. Thurber and a bumbling publishing house (a favorite object of Thurber's ire); "What a Lovely Generalization!" a mock discourse on some peculiarities of American speech; and a witty, five-part series of stories on that strangely American phenomenon, radio soap opera, which was entitled "Soapland." Thurber's blindness-induced attachment to the radio dovetailed neatly with his amused interest in the outrageously attenuated traumas and conundrums afflicting the strong, long-suffering heroines of these romances and their often-ineffectual heroes. In many ways, they reflected his long-held view of the relationship between American men and women – although he never explicitly says so. The men are weak, the women are strong.

Not only was the "Soapland" series a triumph of incisive, straightforward reporting and sociological observation, it demonstrated Thurber's extraordinary ability to absorb a huge amount of factual information gathered for him by others and weave it into a smooth, entertaining narrative. Ironically, as well written as it is, the "Soapland" series, which appeared in *The New Yorker* during the spring and summer of 1948, is strangely archaic as well. The world it describes, both artistic and commercial, unwittingly was on the verge of extinction, soon to be devoured by television – a medium for which Thurber, understandably, had little feeling. "Soapland," as well as Thurber's "Natural History" drawings, found their way into a new collection, *The Beast in Me and Other Animals,* published in the fall of 1948.

The Beast in Me also contained several prime examples of the type of piece that would come to dominate Thurber's later work: word game gymnastics and convoluted comic dialogues. In "Here Come the Tigers," two intoxicated chums barge in on Thurber one night and keep him up to all hours with anagrams that show how a word's "mood and tone" are "echoed in its component parts." One friend chants: "There are lips in pistol / And mist in times, / Cats in crystal, / And mice in chimes." The friends plant further seeds of insomnia by challenging Thurber to find three six-letter words with *tiger* hidden in them. It is dawn before he comes up with them: gaiter, goiter, aigret.

"The Waters of the Moon" is a dialogue piece similar in some ways to a word game but featuring fantastic variations on a literary theme. Both pieces are etymological and literary tours de force and dazzling demonstrations of Thurber's vocabulary and erudition, but in time his obsession with words and language would blunt the edge of his humor.[47]

At this point, however, success begat other enterprises. Although he was horrified by the hash that movie impresario Samuel Goldwyn had made of "The Secret Life of Walter Mitty," which had been released in August 1947, Thurber willingly undertook other commercial ventures. He allowed old drawings to be used in advertisements for bug spray, an aftershave lotion, and a department store, and he agreed to endorse *Webster's New World Dictionary of the American Language*. In the spring of 1949, he complained to one of his attorneys that all of these sidelines were driving up his legal bills: "People began to make ballets, print dresses, fired enamel tea trays, beer coasters, recordings, and oratorios out of the small things I have written and drawn. Writers began to accuse me of plagiarism, invasion of privacy, libel, and unAmerican activities. This is known as success in America."[48]

That Thurber had overcome blindness and mental breakdowns to become America's premier humorist was certified – if certification was required – by his lionization in the July 9, 1951, *Time* magazine cover story for which he had drawn his last cartoon. T. S. Eliot told *Time* that Thurber, his favorite humorist, was the creator of funny stories and drawings that were "also a way of saying something serious."

"There is a criticism of life at the bottom of it. It is serious and even somber. Unlike so much humor, it is not merely a criticism of manners – that is, of the superficial aspects of society at a given moment – but something more profound. His writings and also his illustrations are capable of surviving the immediate environment and time out of which they spring. To some extent, they will be a document of the age they belong to," Eliot said.[49]

Acclaim and honors would come easily now for Thurber; productivity, health, and peace of mind would not.

6

The Uses of Laughter

The late 1940s and early 1950s may have been a period of critical approbation and financial success for Thurber, but he felt far from secure. The pall cast on the literary, artistic, and cultural communities by the postwar Red scare infuriated and depressed him, even though he never was targeted openly by the witch-hunters and was not affected personally by their rabid crusade. Any attack on individual liberty enraged him, and he feared for the safety of something he held especially dear: the country's sense of humor. Comedy, he wrote, "sickens in the weather of intimidation and suppression, and such a sickness could infect a whole nation."[1]

As early as 1946, Thurber found himself embroiled in a teapot turmoil that turned ugly. His old college humor magazine, the *Sundial,* was threatened by the ossifying administrators at Ohio State. They felt the magazine had become too raunchy, as many college periodicals were inclined to do with former servicemen now editing them. The O.S.U. fathers decided to stem this libidinous development by shutting down the magazine for a year and then renaming it *Scarlet Fever.* Thurber and other former *Sundial* editors were outraged at such ham-handed censorship, and Thurber's fury was stoked even further by a letter he got from a university official, who attributed the magazine's supposed decline to "an unhealthy gang of Cleveland Jews [who] got control and, brother, when they get dirty, they don't fool around."[2] Thurber began an intense letter-writing campaign to oppose the *Sundial* shut-down and name-change, enlisting the support of other former editors of the magazine, including Gardner Rea, his *New Yorker* colleague, and Elliott Nugent. The cowed would-be censors at O.S.U. retreated; the name *Sundial* rose again on the magazine's masthead, and the tempest passed.

Within a year, Thurber found himself involved in another public debate over civil liberties when he took umbrage and issue with an editorial in the conservative *New York Herald Tribune,* which proposed on Thanksgiving Day, 1947, that workers be required to sign statements pledging their loyalty to the U.S. government. When E. B. White, Roger Angell, and other well-known writers sent letters to the *Tribune,* denouncing its proposal as unconstitutional, and the paper testily defended its position, Thurber joined the fray. He wrote to the paper that its editorials "could be used as a preface to a book on how to set up a totalitarian state under the bright banner of the security of the nation and the responsibilities of individuals to the Constitution." He suggested that the first chapter of this totalitarian how-to book be entitled "How to Discredit Liberals as Dangerous Elements Who Imperil the Safety of the Nation and the True Meaning of the Constitution, and Who Stand in the Way of the New Freedom and the Greater Security."

"But why should I instruct your editorial writer? He seems to have a natural gift and a peculiar facility for writing the handbook." [3]

Philosophically, Thurber was a vigorous opponent of Communism and long had been; even during the 1930s, when Marxism and the cause of the proletariat were popular among many writers and intellectuals, he publicly ridiculed and criticized them. Nevertheless, his basic, personal conservatism, instilled during a good Victorian upbringing in the Midwest, was constantly at loggerheads with his fiercely liberal attitude toward the civil and First Amendment rights of artists of every stripe. He was particularly distressed by the witch-hunters' assaults on writers, who he felt were a special breed of artist requiring complete freedom. When the self-anointed guardians of the country's safety assembled the names of writers whose work they viewed as subversive and worthy of blacklisting, Thurber was almost sorry not to be included on the roster. "If and when I am listed as an old Bolshevik," he wrote to a friend, "I will at least join the distinguished company of some of the patriotic Americans whom I love and admire."[4] On other occasions, Thurber liked to boast that despite his open and often-expressed scorn for overblown advocates of "Americanism," the would-be superpatriots in the federal government left him alone. "Nobody ever knocked on my door," he told an interviewer in 1958. "Somebody asked a Congressman once – I don't know the Congressman but he's from my state – at a party, 'Why have you never investigated Thurber?' And he said – and this is my proudest medal: 'Because our wives and daughters wouldn't allow it.' I think that's wonderful."[5]

Thurber's delight might have dimmed had he known that J. Edgar Hoover's minions at the Federal Bureau of Investigation indeed did have a file on him, and actually had been keeping tabs on his activities since 1939.[6] He had become suspect because, along with Hemingway, Dashiell Hammett, and dozens of other well-known writers and artists, he was what the Red-hunters later termed "prematurely anti-fascist," having signed protest letters urging aid to the Liberal and Communist-backed Republican forces fighting the Fascists led by Francisco Franco, a protégé of Hitler, in the Spanish Civil War. Thurber's occasional association with other liberal groups kept the FBI's newspaper clippers and filing clerks fitfully on his trail until the early 1950s.

Much of what is in Thurber's FBI file is repetitious, and the roster of those with whom he was linked contains some of the most distinguished names in American arts and letters. A February 1948 *New York Times* story, clipped and preserved in the file along with a report of the California state senate's Committee on Un-American Activities, notes that Thurber joined Oscar Hammerstein II, Moss Hart, Walter Huston, Norman Rockwell, Agnes DeMille, Edna Ferber, and dozens of others on a committee sponsoring a drive to oppose "censorships in the arts" and offering its support to the Hollywood Ten, a group of screenwriters subsequently blacklisted and jailed for refusing to testify before the U.S. House of Representatives' Committee on Un-American Activities (HUAC).[7]

If the fact that Thurber had signed a liberal group's protest letter was mentioned in testimony before HUAC, or his name appeared in such suspect publications as *People's World* or *The Daily Worker,* into his FBI file went a copy of the HUAC committee transcript or the newspaper clipping. That Thurber was reported to be "disgusted" by Elliott Nugent's "red-baiting activities in Equity" is far less astonishing than that such an item surfaced in so bourgeois a feature as a Broadway gossip column written for the Communist *Daily Worker.*[8]

An early entry in Thurber's FBI file obtained through the federal Freedom of Information Act is a list of members of the League of American Writers, which included Van Wyck Brooks, Malcolm Cowley, Dorothy Parker, S. J. Perelman, Lillian Hellman, Irwin Shaw, Upton Sinclair, and Carl Van Doren, as well as Thurber. A "Dear Edgar" note accompanying this list advised the ever-vigilant FBI chief: "Here's a pretty good Directory of Communists." Under restrictions imposed by the Act, the name of Hoover's correspondent is blacked out, and twenty-nine pages of Thurber's file were deleted. The explanations for the deletions given by the Bureau's overworked and regulation-bound bureaucrats range from a legal exemption for "national defense or foreign policy" reasons to an "unwarranted invasion of the personal privacy of another person" and a reluctance to reveal the identity of a confidential informant. If ever valid, all of these reasons for deletion probably have long since been rendered obsolete by the likely demise of everyone involved in the file's compilation and the end of the Cold War atmosphere that prompted its irrational creation.*

Perhaps the most ironic item in Thurber's FBI file can be found in a catalog for an unidentified benefit auction that was scheduled to occur at the Delmonico Hotel in New York on February 19, 1939. Among the signed cartoons Thurber donated for sale was an unpublished drawing, dated 1935 and captioned: "Come on – fall in line, buddy. We're chasing Reds!"

The country's salvation, Thurber felt, lay in its sense of humor. He was fond of quoting the observation of his old Ohio State professor Joseph Taylor: "A thing that cannot endure laughter is not a good thing." Thurber told one interviewer, "Well, there isn't a trace of humor in Communism, is there? I think any political system that vehemently attacks humor reveals a great weakness. . . . One of the great things we have here is humor – even in war. We ought not to lose that." [9]

In a 1952 piece for *The New York Times*, Thurber correctly predicted that the irresponsible anticommunist crusades, such as those of Wisconsin's Republican Senator Joseph R. McCarthy, would eventually be brought down by their own buffoonery – the very fate that befell McCarthy two years later following the televised Army-McCarthy hearings. "Fortunately, this is the country of the horselaugh, the raspberry, and the Bronx cheer," Thurber wrote. "When a democracy be-

---

*An appeal was submitted to the FBI, seeking the deleted pages from Thurber's file, but the FBI, citing a substantial backlog in pending appeals regarding such requests, and time restrictions on those appeals, refused to reply to it in time for publication.

gins to laugh at boogie men, it is no longer in danger of destroying itself." [10]

While the Red scare was in full swing, however, Thurber found humor difficult to write. He continued tinkering fruitlessly with his play about *The New Yorker*, worried that his satiric portrait of a congressman in it might be denounced as un-American, and finally retreated to the safety of fantasy and the past. During a four-month stay in Bermuda in 1950, he wrote another fairy tale, *The 13 Clocks*, which centered on the theme that people need humor as well as love to survive. When the tale's heroic prince rides off in the end with his beloved princess, a well-meaning but inept wizard named Golux advises them wistfully: "Remember laughter. You'll need it even in the blessed isles of Ever After." [11]

As he did in *The White Deer*, Thurber filled *The 13 Clocks* with poetry, puns, funny-sounding nonsense words, reverse limericks, and other word games. The names of his wizard, Golux, and several other characters, Hagga, Pivir, Ninud, Nadal, and Todal, even came from the creaky diplomatic code he had learned during World War I. His villainous duke in *The 13 Clocks* bore a bit of a resemblance to Harold Ross, as did the King in *The White Deer*.[12]

The 13 Clocks again presents the tale of a hero's quest. The cruel duke tries to kill time by stopping all thirteen clocks in his castle. A handsome prince named Zorn, disguised as a minstrel, must accomplish a heroic task, the delivery of a thousand rare gems to the duke, in order to win the hand of the villain's niece, the fair princess, who alone can use the warmth of her hands to restart the frozen clocks. Zorn obtains the gems from a woman who weeps jewels. While the jewels that come from the tears of sadness "last beyond all measure," the jewels that come from the tears of laughter, though they provide "a little pleasure," are fleeting and turn to fluid. Zorn obtains jewels of laughter, enough to win the Princess, and the duke is left with only a puddle to ponder before being slain by the mystical monster, the Todal.

Language, the very sound of words, was becoming increasingly important to Thurber artistically, as it became even more central to his own experience of reality. His use of assonance and alliteration conveys the perilous journey of Zorn with special power: "The brambles and thorns grew thick and thicker in a ticking thicket of bickering crickets. Farther along and stronger, bonged the gongs of a throng of frogs, green and vivid on their lily pads. . . . The pilgrims leaped over the bleating sheep creeping knee-deep in a sleepy stream, in which swift and slippery snakes slid and slithered silkily, whispering sinful secrets." [13]

Thurber's style, like Zorn's journey, was growing "thick and thicker."

Thurber had such fun writing *The 13 Clocks* that he hated to hand it over to the publisher, Simon and Schuster. "In the end they took it away from me, on the ground that it was finished and that I was just having fun tinkering with clocks and running up and down secret stairs. They had me there," he wrote in an introduction to the book, which was splendidly illustrated by Marc Simont, his friend and neighbor in West Cornwall.[14]

Thurber resisted attempts by readers and critics to find deep meaning in *The 13 Clocks*. "I believe that narrative comes first in a fairy tale and I have found that if you start out with a set philosophy in mind the story is likely to become stilted or even pretentious," he wrote to one reader. "All I did was to write a fairy tale whose plot, incidents, and characters interested me, as did the writing. I have no doubt that philosophy is inherent in such an approach and anyone is welcome to read whatever they want into the book. I didn't deliberately put it there." When a critic for the *Hartford Times* sniffed that *The 13 Clocks* was "meaningless," Thurber groused in a letter to friends, "What is the meaning of

Cinderella? I think it must be that if you can ride in a pumpkin without catching pneumonia you are lucky." [15]

Returning himself from the isles of Ever After, Thurber still was disinclined to dock at the port of the present. Instead he resumed work on a series of articles about his forebears, his parents, and other Columbus, Ohio, folk who had exerted important influences on him, including newspapermen he had worked with, professors at Ohio State, and the part-Cherokee, part-Afro-American man who managed a bizarre baseball team for the Columbus Blind Asylum. Initially appearing in *The New Yorker* between 1951 and 1952, these pieces later were published in book form as *The Thurber Album,* the longest single literary effort he had completed up to that time. He labored intensely on it, writing hundreds of letters to dozens of people seeking the background facts that fleshed out his own memories and the reminiscences of others. For all of the details he gathered, however, Thurber deliberately idealized many of the figures he profiled. A few years later, he told George Plimpton and Max Steele of *The Paris Review* that his return to recollections had been a "kind of escape – going back to the Middle West of the last century and the beginning of this, when there wasn't this fear and hysteria. I wanted to write the story of some solid American characters, more or less as an example of how Americans started out and what they should go back to – to sanity and soundness and away from this jumpiness. It's hard to write humor in the mental weather we've had, and that's likely to take you into reminiscence. Your heart isn't in it to write anything funny." [16]

What Thurber hadn't reckoned on was the reaction of his relatives who had been back there in the past with him and didn't like his recollections of it and them. His mother and younger brother, Robert, residing together now in a Columbus hotel, expressed apprehension about Thurber's collective portrait of the family. Robert voiced special

resentment over the profile of Charles Thurber, which Thurber had entitled "Gentleman from Indiana" but which Robert bitterly complained
should have been called "Hoosier Halfwit." [17]

Thurber was shocked and frustrated. His family's insularity infuriated him (Robert was particularly displeased by Thurber's failure to
mention their father's "wonderful penmanship"), and he was miffed
that Robert still willingly cashed checks he sent but now never acknowledged them. But Thurber was distressed by any estrangement
with his family, especially with his aged but feisty mother. He solicited
and collected compliments on the *Album* pieces and forwarded them to
Columbus in an effort to show that others thought highly of the profile
of his father. To E. B. and Katharine White, he wrote that their warm
praise for the profile probably fell on deaf ears as far as his brother
was concerned: "Nothing much can be done with him, I'm afraid, since
he has become a unique hermit in the past forty years, out of touch
with everybody and everything, except his mother. He has no sense
of English or of writing . . . and never reads any books. The life of a
specialist in first editions and those made valuable by errata and failure is distorting. To him Sinclair Lewis's 'Our Mr. Wrenn' is the most
important Lewis book, because of errors in the first run-off. The early
failures of established writers are worth more than their successes. Failures, mistakes, and scarcity make up a strange criterion of value. He
never reads any of his prize items." [18]

Thurber's older brother, William, was less concerned about the
Album's portrait of their father, to whom he had not been as close as
Robert. In Helen Thurber's view, William enjoyed the attention he received by virtue of his younger brother's books — and also appreciated
the regular checks he got from Connecticut. William had a sense of
the absurd that resembled his brother James's, but no writing talent. In

1951, their irrepressible mother told *Time* magazine, "William is twice as crazy as Jamie, only he can't put it down." [19]

The Thurber Album became a best-seller, but the critical reception it received from his family, the narrow-minded provincialism that seemed to embody Columbus, left him bitter. He wrote to a friend: "The emotional debris was terrific, since Columbus is the heart of evasion and fatty degeneration of criticism. Said my mother: 'It wouldn't go down very well with the young man of today if you reported that your grandfather sent a substitute to the Civil War.'" In excavating his past for warm recollections, Thurber unearthed much that he could not stand. "My unfond memories would fill a bucket," he wrote. To E. B. White, Thurber vowed: "I am going to write about imaginary people from now on since real ones take too much out of me." [20] It was a pledge he would let lapse when he began to write about Harold Ross — the project that would cost him not only more anguish, but White's friendship as well.

Thurber had seen a lot of Ross during the editor's last days. Ross, estranged from his third wife, ill with lung cancer, and consequently less involved with editing *The New Yorker,* was living in the Algonquin Hotel, where Thurber and Helen always stayed during extended visits to New York. They spent a good deal of time with Ross, who had always fascinated Thurber and was now, at the very end, becoming a close friend. Thurber was devastated when Ross died suddenly on December 6, 1951, while undergoing surgery to stem his cancer.

The urge to capture Ross's unique personality on paper, long germinating in Thurber's mind, took firm root. "I'm going to do a piece about Ross, but it will take time," he wrote to friends nine days after Ross's death. "He was the principal figure in my career, and I don't know what I would have amounted to without his magazine, in which ninety percent of my stuff has appeared. He was also a great part of my life, and I realize how much I loved him and depended on him. . . . For the first time I have become deeply aware of the chill sweeping across the cold and starry space. . . . Ross was a part of my daily life for almost exactly a quarter of a century. It is always hard to believe that extremely vital people can die. He represented life to me the way few others do." [21]

On the very day Ross died, Thurber also had to deal with yet another matter involving his now not-so-dear alma mater. He wrote a curt but dignified letter to Howard L. Bevis, president of Ohio State, rejecting the offer of an honorary Doctor of Letters degree, citing as the reason for his refusal a recent decision by the O.S.U. administration to impose a gag rule on all campus speakers. Henceforth both outside lecturers and their speeches would have to be reviewed in advance by the university president so as to prevent presentation of any supposedly subversive views. McCarthyites were delighted, but Thurber, only recently triumphant in the *Sundial* brouhaha, was outraged. "I have faith that Ohio State will restore freedom of speech and freedom of research, but until it does I do not want to seem to approve of its recent action," he wrote to the O.S.U. president. "The acceptance of an honorary degree right now would certainly be construed as such approval, or as indifference to the situation." [22]

There was insult, as well as irony, in the standoff with Ohio State. *The Male Animal,* of course, had dealt precisely with such an issue, academic freedom, at a university that patently was based on Ohio State. Now the character of a narrow-minded trustee in the play had been "recreated in the actual body of the chairman of the board," Thurber had written to a friend on the faculty. "This is mighty goddam discouraging." [23] What's more, the honor that O.S.U. proposed to bestow on Thurber was being offered in a decidedly backhanded way: at a less-prestigious December convocation, not the June graduation, and in absentia if he declined to show up. Kenyon College, in Gambier,

Ohio, already had bestowed an honorary Doctor of Letters degree on Thurber in person in its June 1950 commencement, and in June 1951 he had received a Doctor of Humane Letters degree in person from Williams College, in Williamstown, Massachusetts. In June 1953 Yale University would award him an honorary Doctor of Letters degree. Ohio State, from which he had never gotten a regular degree, ended up never awarding him an honorary one, either. It did, however, eventually relax the gag rule that had so offended him. Perhaps most ironic of all, the City Center of New York decided early in 1952 to revive *The Male Animal,* with Elliott Nugent recreating his role as Tommy Turner and Robert Preston assuming the role of the former football hero, Joe Ferguson. It earned rave reviews. Left intact, the play's call for academic freedom was more pointed and pertinent in 1952 than it had been in 1940, and Thurber wound up with an unanticipated windfall in box office receipts.

Despite this success, Thurber was plagued by a persistent depression and what he called a neuritis headache. His melancholy was broken by spells of irrational fury that prompted one old friend to describe him during these fits as "a storming, raging, vituperative madman."[24] Finally his alternating moods of ennui and anger were diagnosed as a toxic thyroid condition. His brother Robert had suffered a similar thyroid imbalance years before and had undergone a thyroidectomy that left him perpetually listless. Thurber, already surgery-shy because of his repeated eye operations, was afraid of a similar outcome if he had his thyroid removed, so efforts were undertaken to correct his problem with medication instead. Several years of therapy were required before a proper combination of drugs and dosage was determined, and throughout the period Thurber and all who encountered him were beset by his sudden outbursts of churlishness.

Thurber did little writing during 1952 and 1953, a period he described in a woeful letter to friends as his "descent into the sewers of the City of Negation. . . . Right now I'm an old torn dollar umbrella stuck in a trash bin and it is beginning to rain." His relationship with *The New Yorker* grew increasingly sour as his comic sense waned. "I can't do anything now since my humor sounds like that of an assistant embalmer," he wrote to Peter De Vries. What pieces he did submit to the magazine – frequently morose and unfunny – were often turned down, which depressed him even more. To his old friend John McNulty he wrote glumly: "I fear that where my fancy flowered and my wild invention grew, there is now a small and arid space. The fresh phrases are wilted and there is rust on my metaphor mixer."[25]

One bright spot for Thurber during this grim period was the marriage of his daughter, Rosemary, to Frederick Sauers. Rosemary, a senior at the University of Pennsylvania studying drama, had met Sauers, then studying at Penn's Wharton School of Finance, when they both took part in a college play. Although like any father of the bride, Thurber grumbled about all the expenses being dumped in his lap, the March 1953 wedding at the Ritz-Carlton in Philadelphia was a great success. "Rosemary looked beautiful, I didn't fall down," he wrote to friends who couldn't attend.[26] Shortly thereafter, he published a new anthology of pieces, *Thurber Country,* which he dedicated to "Rosie and Fred." In time Rosemary presented Thurber with three grandchildren, Sara, Gregory and Mark.

Thurber Country contains some of his best later pieces, including "File and Forget," but its high point is "Do You Want to Make Something Out of It?" perhaps the finest exercise in wordplay he ever wrote. In it he describes Superghosts, a word game in which a player provides the letters at the center of various words and challenges fellow players to extrapolate from this core the complete words wherein it can be found. "The Superghost aficionado is a moody fellow, given to spelling to himself at table, not listening to his wife . . . , wondering why he didn't detect, in yesterday's game, that 'cklu' is the guts of 'lacklustre' and priding himself on having stumped everybody with 'nehe,' the middle of 'swineherd.' "[27]

When Thurber finds himself stumped, however, he often spends sleepless nights conjuring up phantom "bed-words" to fit the mysterious letter cores he has been given. When all he can come up with for *sgra* are *disgrace, crossgrained* and *misgraft,* he produces, in a perfect parody of *Webster's Dictionary,* a wonderful selection of fantasy words, all with the ring of plausibility: "**Kissgranny. 1.** A man who seeks the company of older women, especially older women with money; a designing fellow, a fortune hunter. **2.** An overaffectionate old woman, a hugmoppet, a bunnytalker. **Blessgravy.** A minister or cleric; the head of a family; one who says grace. Not to be confused with praisegravy, one who extols a woman's cooking, especially the cooking of a friend's wife; a gay fellow, a flirt, a seducer. *Colloq.,* a breakvow, a shrugholy. **Fussgrape. 1.** One who diets or toys with his food, a light eater, a person without appetite, a scornmuffin, a shuncabbage. **2.** A man, usually American, who boasts of his knowledge of wines, a smugbottle."[28]

The piece sparked an avalanche of mail from wordplay fanatics, all offering Thurber additional real or fictional entries in the *sgra* sweepstakes, or new riddles to solve. When his old genius burst forth, the public responded with glee.

Despite Thurber's penchant for gloom, all was not bleak in other respects. The Martha Kinney Cooper Ohioana Library Association chose in October 1953 to award him a special Ohio Sesquicentennial Career Medal for the benefits derived by both his native state and the nation from his work. He responded with a graceful speech extolling the power and indispensability of humor, and even tossed a few bouquets to his wayward home town. Delivered in his absence by George

Smallsreed, an old colleague from the *Dispatch* who was now its editor, Thurber's Ohioana speech was as eloquent a discourse on the importance of free expression as anything he ever wrote, and it put McCarthy and his minions on notice that truth, abetted by humor, would bring them down. The American "tradition of rugged and unafraid humor . . . must not be allowed to pass into legend and limbo, out of fear and trembling," Thurber wrote. The nation's tough humor "came over in the *Mayflower,* it flourished in the free American soil, it was carried westward in covered wagons, it was borne upon our battlefields as bright and inspiring as regimental colors. It has been seasick, wagon-weary, and shot full of holes, but it has always managed to survive."

"Let us not forget the uses of laughter or store them away in the attic. . . . Dangerous men . . . are nourished as much by attack as they are by praise. It magnifies their importance, builds them a stately mansion on the front page, and dignifies their meanest motives and their merest shenanigans. Laughter, on the other hand, is often their undoing. It shows them up in a clear and honest light, and drives away the big distorted shadows in which they love to lurk. Many of the perils they flaunt in the shadows are real perils, but they can be dealt with better in the light. Laughter could bring many things out into the open including the true shape and purpose of our Bill of Rights. It was designated as a fortress and a sanctuary, not as a hideout." [29]

As for the hometown and state about which he had a bucketful of unfond memories, Thurber turned benign. "It is a great moment for an Ohio writer living far from home when he realizes that he has not been forgotten by the state he can't forget." His books proved, he said, "that I am never very far away from Ohio in my thoughts, and that the clocks that strike in my dreams are often the clocks of Columbus." [30]

Thurber could not accept the Ohioana award in person because he was looking after Helen, whom he liked to call his seeing-eye wife, following her own frightening encounter with visual trauma. While proofreading the manuscript of *Thurber Country* in August 1953, she suffered a detached retina in her left eye that required emergency surgery. Unable to contact Dr. Bruce, who was vacationing on a remote Colorado ranch and couldn't be reached by telephone, Thurber asked the Associated Press to track him down. Dr. Bruce, thus located, recommended another well-known, New York-based eye doctor for the surgery, which was successful. The publicity surrounding the Thurbers' search for their eye doctor prompted nearly a dozen men, all unknown to the Thurbers, to offer to donate one of their eyes to Helen, anonymously and for nothing. Since a whole eye cannot be transplanted, these were grand but futile gestures that nonetheless touched Thurber greatly. He wrote to George Smallsread, "This kind of thing has increased our love and admiration of the human race."[31]

By the spring of 1955, Thurber and Helen felt well enough to do something they had not done since before World War II: visit Europe. They sailed for France on the *Liberté,* reveled in a Paris untroubled by war clouds, then went on to be lionized once again in London. At last he met his admirer T. S. Eliot, with whom he had a quiet, private tea alone. The British press adored Thurber and dispatched phalanxes of reporters to interview him. As was his practice back home, he almost always agreed to a requested interview. Having been a reporter, he hated to turn one away – and he also loved the attention and publicity. Invariably, Thurber's physical presence impressed reporters who expected him to resemble the meek, retiring men in his cartoons. Instead they found him an imposing figure with a high-pitched, youthful voice, a smooth control of his cigarettes and drinks despite his blindness, and expressive hands whose long, delicate fingers repeatedly riffled his thick, unruly hair. His fingernails were long, tapered, and strong. He could perforate the top of a beer can with the tip of his thumb.[32]

In between the socializing and declaiming, Thurber found time to indulge his fondness for exotica by going up to Scotland to delve into the legend of the Loch Ness Monster. Authorities in Inverness made their archives available to him, and with the aid of a researcher he combed the files in preparation for an article that ultimately appeared in *Holiday* magazine under the title "There's Something Out There!"

After Scotland, Thurber and Helen returned to Paris, where he agreed to talk at length with George Plimpton and Max Steele, then the young editors of the *Paris Review,* for a series that subsequently was published in a book, *Writers at Work*. He came to rue the rambling nature of that discourse, since it ended up receiving far wider distribution and more scholarly scrutiny than his offhand ruminations in England. He wrote to Malcolm Cowley, the editor of *Writers at Work,* "The transcribed interview seems to me a little like 'cold mutton,' as Oscar Wilde described his first experience of sexual intercourse with a woman. As I indicated in my letter to Plimpton, jabber is taking over, and careful writing is disappearing." [33]

Upon Thurber's return from Europe in the fall of 1955, Simon and Schuster published *Thurber's Dogs,* a collection of old articles and drawings that dealt with his incomparable canines, and he continued writing occasional pieces for *The New Yorker,* few of them memorable. He also puttered interminably with several ideas for plays – the one on Ross, one about a congressman, one about the venerable mansion in Bermuda where he and Helen always stayed. Periodically he tried to blend elements of one play into another. He never got it to work.

Thurber had similar problems with a long piece he began in an effort to summarize his beliefs about America's mind and morals in one grand political satire. Originally called "The Spoodle," it started out lambasting the House Committee on Un-American Activities and McCarthyism, then evolved into "The Sleeping Man," a fairy tale satire on the woes that beset middle-aged American men, then became another version of "The Spoodle" entitled "The Grawk," which in turn became "The Nightinghoul." He wanted to write a significant book on the travails of modern American life and simply couldn't complete it.[34]

He had better success mending the family fences in Columbus. He even resumed his old habit of going home for Christmas. His mother was growing increasingly feeble; her "mens is still sano, but her corpus is frail," he had written to his son-in-law early in 1954.[35] In December 1955, only three weeks shy of her ninetieth birthday, Mame Thurber died after a stroke, having lingered for a month as he sat beside her bed.

While he endured the wait for his mother's death, Thurber began writing fables again – grim, biting assaults on human nature in general and the idiocies in contemporary life, as he saw them. These tales, published first in *The New Yorker* during 1956 and later that year as *Further Fables for Our Time,* were in some ways vignettes from the large social satire he was unable to complete. With puns and witty fantasy words as the chief humorous elements in them, these forty-seven new fables took dead aim at political mendacity and human foibles of every sort. As the moral to one tale puts it: "O why should the spirit of mortal be proud, in this little voyage from swaddle to shroud." [36] Time, the inevitability of death, vanity – these are themes that were always present in Thurber's work and now became pervasive. In "The Truth About Toads," the revelers at the Fauna Club boast about their prowess. The Stork, the Raven, the Rooster all tout themselves, and the Toad, not to be outdone, says he has a precious jewel in his head. When he falls asleep, his fellow drinkers have the Woodpecker poke a hole in his skull, but they find there "wasn't anything there, gleaming or lovely or precious." The brutal moral: "Open most heads and you will find nothing shining, not even a mind." [37]

Thurber's new fables, full of tough, conservative moral tenets, were eagerly reprinted in textbooks and earned him the American Library Association's $5,000 award for the piece of imaginative literature that best advanced the causes of liberty and justice.[38]

Back home, Thurber maintained an active nocturnal social life, his disabilities and periodic depression notwithstanding. One friend in Connecticut recalled how Thurber seemed to blossom and become "super-alive" as the night progressed, "offering to his friends not just conversation but a complete show – talking in every form of American dialect," reciting "fifty completely original limericks," trying out ideas for pieces he planned to write.[39]

Physically, he remained a formidable figure. Peter De Vries likened him to a giant praying mantis, about whose "elongated form there hovered the same air of something delicate and improbable, of almost eerie sensitivity, of tactile grace and predatory caution."[40] A reporter from *Newsweek* found "a touch of powerful authenticity in the sight of James Thurber, his hair tumbling over his forehead, raising his 6 feet 1 ½ inches awkwardly from a chair and flopping his long arms about like a scarecrow in Hydra-Matic drive, as he duplicates the nasal platform delivery of long-dead Ohio politicians."[41]

Since Thurber now was unable to see how the words and phrases he planned to use in a piece might look on a page, he needed listeners, one friend observed. He also loved performing, and frequently would make himself the butt of his humor, as he often had done in print. Sports columnist Red Smith recalled how Thurber, reaching for his cocktail at a party, knocked over two drinks in succession and then promptly "sprang to his feet and delivered an impassioned protest to an imaginary House Rules Committee about the untidy habits of this member Thurber, who persistently loused up the club premises on the flimsy pretense, the hollow excuse, that he was blind."

"His witty eloquence made it funny, and like all his humor, it was also bitterly poignant," Smith wrote.[42]

In 1957 Thurber produced two more books, and reached a significant personal and professional milestone. *Alarms and Diversions* was yet another anthology of previously published articles and distantly drawn cartoons, plus a number of current sober, reflective pieces on contemporary issues. He was so determined to be accorded respect as a serious thinker and commentator that he took to denigrating his earlier, humorous work, dismissing it as unimportant and forgettable. Ultimately, he even denounced daydreaming, in essence renouncing Walter Mitty. He ridiculed those who retreated from reality by engaging in nostalgia or fanciful reveries and insisted that he applied his own imagination to productive ends. He told the Associated Press: "When I sit silent at parties, I am not remembering the time, at my thirteenth birthday party, when I kissed a little girl named Eva, or my election in 1913 as president of the senior class at East High School in Columbus, Ohio, or the evening I got a zither in the rotation pool tournament. At such moments of obliviousness I am trying to write something new, and not under the name of A. I. Glatson (try spelling that backward)."[43] He told another interviewer that he hated having his humor described as "mild and gentle," adding, "I'm lying in wait for the next person that calls me elfin. If it's a man, I'll propose to kick him to death."[44]

Yet he could no more change the natural course of his creative juices than alter the flow of the Scioto River through Columbus. The other book he published in 1957 was *The Wonderful O*, a long fable about a pirate named Black who lands on a quiet isle named Ooroo while looking for jewels and imposes his tyrannical rule on the inhabitants. In the process, he bans the letter O and all words containing it. He loathes O in any form, his mother having become so wedged in a porthole that "we couldn't pull her in so we had to push her out." In prohibiting the use of O, Black tries to rid the island of love and hope, valor and freedom.

Catherine McGehee Kenney calls *The Wonderful O* "the purest Thurber," with words and their meaning the centerpiece of the entire story. Language came to represent life itself to Thurber, and when language was crippled or killed, life suffered the same fate.[45] A sprightly parable against censorship, *The Wonderful O* does at times become a tiresome word game – a source of amusement that was turning into an alarming obsession for Thurber. Yet it nevertheless is a funny book and was well received. Thurber proudly informed his old friend William Shirer on New Year's Eve 1957 that with the publication of these two volumes, *The Wonderful O* and *Alarms and Diversions,* he had now written more books since he had gone blind than when he could see. "A tribute to his guts," Shirer wrote in his diary.[46]

Thurber's pride and his increasing distrust of others were also formidable. He was convinced *The New Yorker* had rejected some of his new fables not because they were less well-written than the others but because the editors found them too potent politically, an accusation the magazine denied. His anger increased when *The New Yorker* ultimately declined to publish *The Wonderful O* because Thurber wouldn't approve the magazine's condensation of the story and he couldn't cut it enough himself to suit the editors. In a letter describing how he thought *The New Yorker* should go about condensing *The Wonderful O*, Thurber mocked the note often placed at the end of *New Yorker* book reviews: " 'The Heart of Darkness,' by Joseph Conrad, was first printed in this magazine in a shorter version under the title 'The Aorta of Darkness.' "[47] His complaints about the changes in *The New Yorker* since Ross's death, a frequent private gripe, now became a public refrain. "We have got into a thing that Ross dreaded all his life – the magazine is getting grim and long," he later told a British interviewer. "It's now a great big business over there – writing and editing – it's terrific. All of us worry about its size, wealth and what I call its 'matronly girth' – but it lacks comedy." [48]

As one who had been a beau of the matronly magazine in her slim, lighthearted youth, Thurber had long wanted to preserve on paper his memories of what she and her incredible father, H. W. Ross, had been like. For years he had labored unsuccessfully on a play about Ross, and similarly nothing had come of a projected book in which he, E. B. White, and four other *New Yorker* veterans had planned to write individual recollections of their vexing but venerated editor. By 1954 Thurber had decided to do his own series of magazine articles on Ross, endeavoring to elucidate the inexplicable. Ross was, he had written to the radio comedian Fred Allen, "one of those rare guys who, when they can't do it at all, can do it better than anyone else." [49] He had let the Whites and others know that he was preparing to go ahead alone on the project, but although several magazines, including *The Atlantic, Harper's,* and *Esquire,* expressed interest in it, other work got in the way. Charles Morton, editor of *The Atlantic,* was more persistent, however, and continued to press Thurber for the Ross articles. In the end, succumbing to Morton's importunings early in 1957, Thurber began work on the pieces, hoping that by finally capturing the elusive essence of Ross in some articles, he later could transfer it to the stage. He also wanted to demonstrate anew what he saw as his own central role in creating *The New Yorker.*

Even though the articles were for another magazine, *The New Yorker,* with some trepidation, offered complete cooperation. Thurber was given an office, a secretary, and carte blanche to use the magazine's library, fact-checking department, and files on Ross. Other old hands at the magazine, including E. B. and Katharine White, Wolcott Gibbs,

Frank Sullivan, Clifton Fadiman, S. J. Perelman, Ogden Nash, and A. J. Liebling, generously supplied letters of reminiscence. White even contributed a brief, bright story about teaching Ross to drive – "Ross at the Wheel" – which Thurber wove into the book's narrative. Additional anecdotes were offered willingly by such diverse Ross friends as Groucho and Harpo Marx, former heavyweight champion Gene Tunney, and Alistair Cooke.

The ten-part series, called "The Years with Ross," began appearing in *The Atlantic* in November 1957 and continued in each issue of the magazine through August 1958. In May 1959, Atlantic, Little, Brown published an expanded version of the pieces in a book. The 310-page tome turned out to be the hefty work Thurber had long wanted to write and had, almost inadvertently, accomplished at last. It also was the most controversial book he ever wrote.

"*The New Yorker* doesn't have to worry about this project, because it rises out of love and devotion," Thurber had written to White in the summer of 1957, "but the righter I get it the crazier it sounds." He later told an interviewer that the secretary to whom he was dictating the book once asked, "Are you sure you're not making this up?" Ross's peccadillos did not require invention, but many who had known him better than Thurber felt his would-be biographer overlooked much of the genius in Ross in order to emphasize the eccentric.[50]

As befits a semimemoir, *The Years with Ross* featured Thurber as a central figure, but he apparently padded his role a bit, appointing himself to a managing editorship he never held, assigning himself duties that he never performed, such as scheduling the production of the magazine and signing its payroll, and describing himself as a regular participant in the weekly meetings of the art staff that he actually attended infrequently. He also seemed to counterbalance every expression

of admiration and praise for Ross with examples of his ignorance, gulli-
bility, or ineptitude. Ross, he wrote, was "by far the most painstaking,
hairsplitting detail-criticizer the world of editing has known," but he
also was "unembarrassed by his ignorance of the great novels of any
country," had a mind "uncluttered by culture," and yet had "the clear-
est concentration of any editor in the world" and possessed a "magic
gift" for surrounding himself with some of the best talent in America
"despite his own literary and artistic limitations."[51] He was devoted to
the proper use of English, read the dictionary like a novel, yet his "spelling was grotesque," he "simply was not a *New Yorker* writer" himself,
and was a "coward" when dealing with some employees, whom he
paid poorly, Thurber wrote.[52] Thurber insisted that his portrait of Ross
was "affectionate," but he candidly acknowledged that his conclusions
about his old editor were "at best, only one man's footnotes, personal
and debatable."[53] And hotly debated they were.

The critical reaction to *The Years with Ross* was largely laudatory
and sales of it were brisk. It became a Book-of-the-Month Club selection, remained on the best-seller list for months, and went through
seven editions. Groucho Marx wrote to Thurber that he had done "a
great job on a very peculiar man"; George S. Kaufman wrote that one
chapter that originally appeared in *The Atlantic* was "the best piece
ever written by anybody about anybody at any time," and others praised
the book with equal enthusiasm.[54]

One place it was decidedly unpopular, however, was at *The New
Yorker* itself, where a delight in puncturing others' pretensions was
not often matched with a thick skin of its own. Thurber later complained to Edmund Wilson that *The New Yorker* had "always dished
it out with laughter and taken it back with tears." While a number of
longtime staffers, including Edmund Wilson, Frank Sullivan, St. Clair

McKelway, and Peter De Vries, enjoyed Thurber's reminiscences of Ross, many others found the book to be a self-centered recollection that belittled its subject in order to elevate its author. Hobart Weekes, one of the editors, told Heywood Hale Broun that a lot of people at the magazine were "very upset by that book," as was Broun himself at the time. (Ross and Thurber both had been friends of his father, newspaper columnist Heywood Broun.) "I thought *The Years with Ross* was a very mean-spirited book, in that it was always saying, 'Hey, what a crazy guy,' and then telling stories, presumably with hearty good humor, which made Ross look like a horse's ass." [55]

Philip Hamburger, a *New Yorker* writer since 1939 and a self-proclaimed "worshipper of Ross," whom he calls "an authentic genius," believes Thurber's portrait didn't do Ross "full justice, in the sense that there was always the slight hint that Ross didn't know what the hell he was doing. There was always this suggestion that maybe [*The New Yorker*'s success] was just an accident, or even some kind of flying blind or intuition . . . , that he just groped his way through." This, in Hamburger's view, was a serious misreading of the man. "Ross was impulsive and wild and wonderful and funny, but he knew what he was doing when he founded that magazine, and he set the pace. I don't want to get into amateur psychology, but I think Thurber both admired and envied him. And I think there is a sense of envy in that book."

In some basic way, Hamburger believes, Thurber "just didn't understand Ross" and couldn't fully grasp "the protean qualities" that made him such a unique figure, a man as at ease with Ginger Rogers or Harpo Marx as with presidential adviser Robert Lovett and New York Mayor William O'Dwyer. [56]

No one disputed the accuracy of the anecdotes about Ross with which Thurber regaled his readers. That Ross was unfamiliar with many literary classics – once asking, for example, "Is Moby Dick the whale or the man?" [57] – was never disputed. And Thurber's re-creation of Ross's quirky, shotgun speech was considered pitch-perfect. It was the overall effect of the portrait that Thurber drew of Ross, and of his own role in the development of *The New Yorker,* that many deemed distorted.

Another *New Yorker* veteran, Roger Angell, the son of Katharine White and stepson of E. B. White, thinks Thurber consciously chose to skew his depiction of Ross in order to show "that he, Thurber, had saved him, and really contributed to his great success." Angell believes that Ross deliberately adopted the guise of "a country boy from Boulder, Colorado, and the reason he did that was because this allowed him to become a great editor. For everything he read, he said, 'You've got to make it clear to me. I don't know anything. I'm a country boy from Boulder, Colorado.' And this was the tone of his famous comments. . . . For some reason, Thurber, I think, *consciously* misunderstood that, and presented Ross as a rube who didn't know what he was doing, which was totally wrong." [58]

No matter how gratifying Thurber may have found the critics' praise for the Ross book or the revenues he received from it, the approval he wanted more than anything was that of E. B. White. He was not to get it. Both White and his wife Katharine, who as a longtime fiction editor at *The New Yorker* had herself been a close colleague of Ross's, were displeased with the book. They thought Thurber's account of how Ross ran *The New Yorker* and paid his writers was inaccurate, as was Thurber's assessment of the editorial role he himself played at the magazine. They also felt the description of Ross's sexual prudery and phobias was distasteful and inaccurate. Years later, the Whites' views on *The Years with Ross* were more tempered, but at the time the *Atlantic* articles appeared and the book was published they were considerably distressed by it, and their close relationship with Thurber essentially ended.[59]

Thurber wrote White a long defense of the book in December 1958, five months prior to its official publication, citing the praise he had received from others for it, just as he had once sent his brother Robert the praise he had received from the Whites for the profile of his father. He vowed that the Ross project would be the last one he would ever do "about real persons, living or dead." [60] But White found this and Thurber's other letters of the time condescending, despite their repeated professions of affection and admiration. It seemed to White that Thurber was trying to show he was as good as or better than White, and to earn his praise at the same time.[61] The two men would see little of each other afterward.

The warm critical applause accorded *The Years with Ross* in this country was not duplicated in Great Britain, much to Thurber's consternation. English critics such as Kenneth Tynan, whom Thurber had once championed, and Dame Rebecca West gave the book a chilly reception. Buffoonery, Dame Rebecca noted icily, was in the eye of the beholder.

In part, Thurber was stunned and stung by the unfavorable British reviews because only a year earlier he had been feted in London as had no other American writer since Mark Twain. In July 1958, the editors of *Punch* magazine, the then-indestructible comic weekly, had not only asked him to join them at their traditional Wednesday lunch, itself an honor, but also invited him to inscribe his initials on the surprisingly flaky wood of their aged luncheon table, where the likes of William Makepeace Thackeray and other British notables had left their marks. It was a privilege previously offered to only one other American, Twain himself. As David Thomas, the last editor of *Punch*, put it, this was an opportunity the magazine accorded only to guests "whose presence [honoured] us as much as we [could] possibly honour them." * [62]

The *Punch* lunch, a wonderful all-night party at the London home of expatriate harmonica virtuoso Larry Adler (whose political black-listing back home was something a determined Thurber later helped to end), and an extraordinary evening with Adlai Stevenson in the Paris apartment of a mutual friend, had made Thurber's five-month 1958 European visit one of his most memorable trips abroad. He felt suitably appreciated there, if not, in his view, sufficiently honored in his native land.

Honors were not to be entirely absent in the United States. In 1959, Thurber returned to Columbus to receive the Distinguished Service Award of the Press Club of Ohio; in 1960, he made another trip home at the behest of Ohio State University, which asked him to dedicate Denney Hall, a new building for the College of Arts and Sciences, named for Joseph Villiers Denney, one of his favorite professors.[63] He was pleased by these tributes in his birthplace, but at the time his sights were set, irrationally, on Stockholm: He told Edmund Wilson that what he really thought he deserved was the Nobel Prize.[64]

He had become, in the view of some of his oldest friends, vain and pompous, a humorist whose sense of humor had largely evaporated in the heat of self-importance or been submerged in alcohol and alienation. At parties he talked incessantly, insisted on being the center of attention, smoked cigarettes constantly and sometimes set fire to the furniture, himself, or others with errant matches or ashes.[65] A young John Updike, meeting Thurber in London in 1958, was aghast at how

---

*Following Thurber, Thomas reported, two other Americans were given "the *Punch* hammer and chisel" to etch their names in the luncheon table: cartoonist Bud Handlesman, also a longtime contributor to *The New Yorker,* and satirist P. J. O'Rourke.

a writer he once idolized had become a terrific bore. "Though Thurber cocked his head alertly at my poor fawning attempts to make conversation, these attempts did not appreciably distract him from the anecdotes of Columbus, Ohio, he had told a thousand times before, and I had read ten years before, in their definitive, printed version," Updike recalled in a 1968 piece for *The New York Times* on writers he had met. "Pages of *The Thurber Album* and *My Life and Hard Times* issued from his lips virtually intact." [66] Angering easily, Thurber often argued furiously with old friends and smashed glasses against the nearest wall.

"He was a tortured man, no doubt about it," Roger Angell says. "To be blind and angry and alcoholic and old is a combination that no one should go through. Add fame to that, and it's a terrible burden. I don't think any of us knows how we would do any better than he did." [67]

Rosemary Thurber does not believe her father was an alcoholic, although "he abused alcohol at times," as do many people. She also doesn't think he was "any more unbalanced than any other well-rounded person." She feels his anger and frustration stemmed from his annoyance "with just the way human beings do their stuff" and his anguish over "not being truly free to just easily come and go and do" because of his blindness. [68]

But more was behind Thurber's loss of perspective and humor than just a case of inflated ego or frequent intoxication, and both he and those closest to him realized it. Despite medication, his thyroid problem occasionally resurfaced; and as his battle with the bottle continued, some of his faculties were beginning to fade and he sensed it. To a friend who found him sitting wearily over brunch in the Algonquin one day, hung over and depressed, he said, "You can't believe what's happening to me." He became preoccupied with thoughts of death, and of the old friends and colleagues who had died: Benchley, Heywood Broun, Ross, John McNulty, Wolcott Gibbs. Sitting in the dining room at the

Algonquin, he would speak of them as ghosts, having lunch at nearby tables.[69] Once able to jest about his own supposed encounter with a specter in "The Night the Ghost Got In," by 1959 he fervently insisted that he indeed had experienced a genuine "supernatural phenomenon," that he long had possessed extrasensory perception and had performed "unbelievable feats of mental telepathy," that the years of sight he had enjoyed despite his damaged eye had been a "miracle."[70]

What perhaps was truly miraculous is that despite the toxic thyroid, the alcohol, the creeping arteriosclerosis and mental aberrations, Thurber still was capable of being productive, articulate, even charming. The 1950s, born under the cloud of McCarthyism, darkened by his growing sense of estrangement from *The New Yorker,* nevertheless were ending for him in a glow of bright hope: He had another Broadway show in the works. The curtain, poised to descend, was not quite ready to be rung down yet.

7

Encore and Exit

In 1959, a television soap opera actress and Thurber devotee named Haila Stoddard hit upon a bold but simple plan for fulfilling her dream of becoming a theatrical producer: She would turn her favorite Thurber pieces into sketches and stage a revue. Incredibly, with luck and the enthusiastic cooperation of Thurber, she not only pulled it off but also enabled him to fulfill a pet Mittyism of his own – a starring role for himself on Broadway.

Thurber had rejected earlier overtures to adapt his stories for the stage, believing that it could not be done successfully. His resistance to the concept weakened, however, as his ability to create new projects waned. Stoddard had shown her script outline to Elliott Nugent, who was impressed and recommended it to Thurber; once Thurber gave his assent to the concept, Stoddard moved with amazing swiftness. She approached a friend, Helen Bonfils, a newspaper heiress in Colorado, for financial backing and quickly got it; Burgess Meredith, an old friend of Thurber's, agreed to direct the show; Tom Ewell, Peggy Cass, Paul Ford, John McGiver, and Alice Ghostly agreed to star; Don Elliott and his jazz quartet were tapped to provide the music.[1]

Into the potpourri were poured dramatizations of "The Secret Life of Walter Mitty," "Mr. Prebel Gets Rid of His Wife," "The Pet Department," "If Grant Had Been Drinking at Appomattox," "The Macbeth

Murder Mystery," "Casuals of the Keys," "File and Forget," "The Unicorn in the Garden," "The Little Girl and the Wolf," "The Wolf at the Door," and "Gentlemen Shoppers," a new piece Thurber wrote for the show; a recitation of "The Night the Bed Fell"; a slide presentation of "The Last Flower"; and "Word Dance," featuring versions of the captions from old Thurber cartoons, recited by twirling actors.[2]

Regardless of how faithful or distorted the adaptations were of Thurber's classics, the project revitalized the man it sought to celebrate. Thurber wrote reams of new material for the revue, very little of it usable; he and Helen hovered over the rehearsals, and when the time came to tour with the tryout production, along he went with that, too. Christened *A Thurber Carnival*, the revue had a gala opening on January 7, 1960, in Columbus's Hartman Theater, where Thurber's old Scarlet Mask Club shows had been performed four decades earlier. He had insisted on an Ohio debut, saying he wanted the show to prove itself in the heart of "Thurber Country."[3] The governor of Ohio decreed James Thurber Week; the mayor of Columbus bestowed the city's first Distinguished Son Award on Thurber, and the critics were indulgent. After three more nights, the show hit the road for a six-week shakedown tour of the Midwest during the dead of winter. It was quite an ordeal for an ill, blind, sixty-five-year-old man to endure, but Thurber persevered with Helen's constant help. After further tryouts in Detroit, Cleveland, St. Louis, Cincinnati, and Pittsburgh, with all the attendant revisions and rewrites, *A Thurber Carnival* opened in Broadway's ANTA Theatre on February 26, 1960, to critical and public applause. Thurber was, for one last time, the king of the Great White Way.[4]

Unfortunately, the critics' raves somehow failed to spark an avalanche of ticket sales, and an actors' strike compelled the box office to close after just seventeen weeks. A month later, the revue reopened in the Central City, Colorado, opera house owned by the show's patron,

Helen Bonfils, and did brisk business during the month of August. It returned to New York in September, but ticket sales the second time around were anemic. Anxious to be of assistance any way he could, Thurber asked Haila Stoddard what she thought he might do and her reply delighted him: Join the show and play yourself. The frustrated author "J. Thurber" in the "File and Forget" sketch henceforth would be portrayed by that frustrated ham, J. Thurber, in person.[5]

Thurber adored being on stage. Sitting in an armchair, his blindness no impediment, he loved to declaim lines he had written — and often mischievously ad lib embellishments. His part-time secretary during the tryout tours, actress Elinor Wright, simply assumed the role of his on-stage secretary as he fussed and fumed and "dictated" letters to the bumbling Charteriss Publishing Company. For three months, through eighty-eight performances, he was in top form. "I consider myself a professional writer, a semi-professional cartoonist, and an amateur actor," he wrote in *The New York Times Magazine*.[6] He claimed that he now planned to create a part for himself in the play about Ross he was forever writing.

Old friends came to see the revue and drop by backstage afterward. His erstwhile girlfriend Ann Honeycutt showed up, as did E. B. White, now distant but magnanimous. Thurber was in constant demand for interviews on radio and television and in the papers. He even managed to finish the final articles for what would be his last collection of pieces, *Lanterns and Lances*. "I will be sixty-six in December," he wrote to friends that fall, "but feel forty-three years younger. . . . I am no longer called 'Old Totters,' but Junior, or Buster, by the older members of Equity."[7]

Regrettably, the novelty of Thurber on stage could not boost ticket sales indefinitely. The show closed in November 1960. Broadway's elite gave him a special Antoinette Perry ("Tony") Award for distinguished writing, but suddenly he found himself back in Connecticut, the spotlights turned off, the applause silenced, the revel ended.

Not long after *Carnival* closed, another of Thurber's secretaries, Fritzi Von Kuegelen, saw him become so agitated and red-faced while dictating something that she thought his head might burst like a balloon. Other longtime friends witnessed subsequent incidents that they later realized had probably signaled the small strokes he began experiencing. He became increasingly violent and abusive, hurling insults at Helen and even more glasses at the wall. Some old friends began avoiding him; others, like Mark Van Doren, were driven away by invective. One evening in 1961, Van Doren, hearing Thurber's umpteenth account of the "true" story behind "The Night the Ghost Got In," twitted him on the tale and got a furious torrent of shouts and threats in return. He realized, too late, that Thurber now passionately believed in the existence of that ghost and found nothing funny in any jests about it.[8]

Thurber's sense of humor was withering, and he seemed to know it. "I am no longer as 'Thurberish' as I used to be," he told one friend.[9] In the foreword to *Lanterns and Lances,* he virtually conceded that he was not writing as many light, funny pieces as before, even though a nation locked in a cold war might benefit from them. He offered no apology for the seriousness of some recent articles, and wanly hoped readers would find others of them in "a humorous vein."

"Every time is a time for comedy in a world of tension that would languish without it. But I cannot confine myself to lightness in a period of human life that demands light. . . . We all know that, as the old adage has it, 'It is later than you think'. . . , but I also say occasionally: 'It is lighter than you think.' In this light, let's not look back in anger, or forward in fear, but around in awareness."[10]

With tepid humor, tiresome word games, a litany of gripes and grumblings, and little light, these late pieces cast a dim glow.

Thurber began yet another lengthy project destined for oblivion, as were his play about Ross and his hefty, unfinished satire now called *The Nightinghoul,* a cautionary tale about the panic that attends phantom dangers, in this case a flying mechanical monster that supposedly threatens a metropolis. His new work, tentatively and alternately entitled "Yesterday Upon the Stair," "What Happened to Me," and "Autobiography of a Mind," sought to explore what he believed were the mysteries of his own psyche: his phenomenal memory, the "total recall" of which he often boasted, his supposed skill at mental telepathy, and the remarkable powers of extrasensory perception he felt he possessed. He also planned to incorporate in this hodgepodge a study of Houdini, some ghost stories, and a detailed account of his "miracle" eye. All of this somehow would address and dismiss the demons now plaguing him. He confided to Elliott Nugent: "This will be the real truth, for the first time. I can't hide any more behind the mask of comedy that I've used all my life. People are not funny; they are vicious and horrible – and so is life!" [11]

Thurber's own life seemed to grow grimmer. *The New Yorker* turned down more of his casuals, and he came to view the rejections as evidence of a great editorial conspiracy against him. "I am afraid you are all now compulsive collaborators and that only psychiatry could cure it," he wrote to Roger Angell. [12] As bad luck would have it, Angell had become Thurber's new editor at the magazine, and Thurber could not stand having his articles scrutinized and then rejected by someone he still considered a kid.

Angell recalls that when he joined *The New Yorker* as a fiction editor in 1956, "one of the people I was given as a writer right away was Thurber, and I thought that was because I knew him. But I realized later it was because he had used up the good will of a number of other editors, I believe, and so they said, 'Well, let's give him to Angell.' I thought this was a compliment. And then I realized it was not so great a compliment as all that." Unfortunately, although Thurber showed tremendous and admirable tenacity by continuing to submit pieces to the magazine, most of them weren't very good and, under *The New Yorker*'s stern policy of requiring every article "to stand or fall on its own merits," they were rejected. While Ross's successor, William Shawn, "very much wanted to keep Thurber in our pages, and certainly all of us . . . wanted humor more than anything else," the bulk of Thurber's later pieces simply "weren't very funny," Angell recalls. "They were strained and they were often querulous. They were the writings of an older person who found life increasingly difficult, who was angry about a great many things happening around him." [13]

The rejections did not improve Thurber's temper. Most of his contact with Angell was over the telephone, and the conversations were not pleasant. "He would submit [an article] and then I would call him up and tell him, with great pleasure, that we were taking the piece, or, with great trepidation, and . . . sadness, that we weren't. And I remember more than once he said to me, 'Do you know who I am?' And I said, 'Yes, Jim, I know who you are.' And he said, 'Do you know I'm the person who . . .' and then he'd tell me his credentials, which seemed pathetic — and irritating. . . . I don't think he really believed we should take something because of somebody's credentials. But he would say, 'Do you know I'm the only person since Mark Twain to be invited to lunch at the long table at *Punch*,' or whatever, and I'd say, 'Yes, Jim, I know that.' That was neither here nor there — but I couldn't say that. And I remember Shawn once saying to me, 'Have you been having a lot of trouble with Thurber?' And I said, 'Yes, I have.' And he said, 'Do you think he's crazy?' And I said, 'Well, yes, I think he is crazy. I don't think he's dangerously crazy, but he was clearly not himself.'" [14]

When Thurber had been himself, he was uniquely funny. Now he had lost the touch – and his way. Angell, who constantly urged him, "Please send us the next piece, please send us the next piece," recognized how daunting a task Thurber faced. "Writing is very, very hard. It's hard to maintain quality. Every writer who has gone about his work seriously and done it for a period of time comes to recognize this. There is no surcease; there is no release from the difficulty of writing. And maybe Jim thought he had reached the position where he could get around this. He could be relieved of the difficulty of writing and it would be easy for him and he would be wonderfully rewarded at the end for everything he wrote. I don't know, that's just a guess. And . . . he was doing an even more difficult thing, which is trying to be funny. It's hard to be funny on a consistent basis for anyone, and I think it's hard to be funny late in life. Not many humorists go on writing after they pass fifty . . . , and those who do are not very funny, it seems to me."

"He didn't have another way to go. . . . He was stuck with this, and people looked for more Thurber, so the . . . problem for him was he was competing with himself. He had an extraordinary reputation – maybe not as large as he wanted it to be or expected it to be, but he knew how good he had been, and it's very hard to keep up with that."[15]

On January 20, 1961, in the wake of the snowstorm that turned John F. Kennedy's inauguration that day into a winter spectacular, Thurber and Helen boarded the *Queen Elizabeth* for what turned out to be a disastrous visit to England. They went in hopes of arranging a London production of *A Thurber Carnival,* even though no commitments had been made to put one on and no British actors had been lined up to perform in it. Thurber insisted that the trip be made, and then desperately sought to back out of it just as they were about to board the ship. His ambivalence was not a good augury.[16]

Once in England, they made little headway on a London version of the revue. The performers who were available seemed unsuitable;

the would-be producer balked; the project foundered; Thurber was depressed and dismayed. He began taking tranquilizers, giving innumerable crotchety interviews, and writing letters full of despair to friends. "It must be better on some other planet! . . . We have gone through seven stages of hell here, the latest being acute homesickness, and we want to get the hell out of here." [17]

But they hung on, with Thurber exhibiting even more alarming symptoms of what Helen called his paranoia. He would stay awake most of the night, ranting aloud, and during the day he repeatedly lashed out at everything and everybody, especially his wife. In May, all plans for a London production of the *Carnival* fell through, and the Thurbers returned home, where for a while tranquility prevailed. He seemed restored to a more or less even keel and was once again capable of writing chatty, amusing notes to friends. "I am pulling out of the deepest Angst I have had since the summer of 1941, when I cracked up after my fifth eye operation," he wrote to E. B. White in June 1961. He added in a playful postscript reminiscent of the old Thurber: "If the United States had had you and G. B. Shaw working together, would the country have had the E.B.G.B.'s? If so, it would have been good for us." [18]

While he believed his depression was abating, or he chose to overlook it, Thurber adamantly refused to acknowledge that something now was wrong with him neurologically. In the familiar surroundings of his home or his usual Algonquin hotel suite, he began bumping into chairs and tables he had deftly avoided before. He often lost control of his bladder and began wetting himself and chairs at parties. In July 1961, he admitted to Edmund Wilson that he had been experiencing "vastations," a word Henry James had used to describe blackouts, but he refused to see a neurologist.[19] Perhaps he knew exactly what a brain specialist would find and was afraid confirmation of it would only hasten his fate. He did reluctantly agree to see his old ophthalmologist, Dr. Gordon Bruce, who was saddened by his decline and surprised that he hadn't had a major stroke yet. When a psychiatrist and the doctor who had treated his thyroid problem suggested he see a neurologist, Thurber vehemently refused. He began to denounce his friends in West Cornwall, and late that summer he demanded that Jap Gude drive him to New York so he could be free of his overpowering dependence on Helen. Drinking heavily, making glum telephone calls to some old friends and meeting morosely with others, he soon wearied of his empty freedom and returned to Connecticut early in September. When he seemed to grow even more irrational and abusive, Helen decided he would be happier in New York and moved them both back to the Algonquin.[20]

On October 3, 1961, the Thurbers attended the Broadway opening of a new Noel Coward musical, *Sail Away,* and then went to a large, loud dinner party to celebrate the occasion at Sardi's East. Thurber clearly was uncomfortable and confused, at one point asking a dinner companion to have Coward come over to greet him just after Coward already had done so. When Coward finished giving a brief speech to the 400 or so guests, Thurber got up and insisted he be given the microphone, much to the embarrassment of many there. He then sang two songs that meant a lot to him – "Who" and "Bye-Bye Blackbird" – but which made no sense that evening. Abruptly, he stumbled and began to totter over. Haila Stoddard's son helped steady him and lead him back to his table. Most of those present assumed he was simply drunk. Helen asked Stoddard's husband, Whitfield Connor, to drive them back to the Algonquin right away. Thurber stayed awake until 4 A.M., shouting at Helen. Finally, they went to bed. At 6 A.M., apparently while on his way to the bathroom, Thurber collapsed, striking his head as he fell. Helen awoke at the noise and discovered him lying in a puddle of blood. An ambulance was summoned and he was taken to Doctors Hospital.[21]

Briefly regaining consciousness at the hospital, Thurber, who disliked most doctors, asked for his old college fraternity brother Dr. Virgil Damon, who had delivered Rosemary. Damon examined him and diagnosed either a cerebral hemorrhage or a brain tumor. Immediate surgery was required. Helen sought to encourage Thurber with his grandfather's rallying cry, "Show your Fisher." Thurber grinned. He underwent brain surgery later that day. The surgeon removed a large, blood-filled tumor found near the speech-control center of Thurber's brain. He also spotted signs of previous small strokes and arteriosclerosis. The outlook was bleak. Thurber lapsed into a coma, rallying only on brief occasions over the next four weeks. Once, Rosemary heard him mutter, "God . . . God . . . God." Later, Helen thought she heard him mumble what may have been his last words: "God bless . . . God damn." He contracted pneumonia and developed a blood clot in a lung.[22]

Thurber had always enjoyed joking, "When I'm on my deathbed, Helen will be at the hairdresser's." He was eerily prescient. Helen indeed was having her hair done when she got a call from Doctors Hospital on the afternoon of November 2, telling her that Thurber was fading fast. By the time she arrived at his bedside, he was gone.[23]

Thurber had not wanted to be buried at Columbus's Green Lawn Cemetery, where, he wrote to friends in 1959, "my once bickering, but now silent, family occupies a good square mile of space."[24] But that really was where he belonged. On November 8, 1961, a bronze urn containing his ashes was interred there, amid the remains of the formerly fractious Thurbers and Fishers. On the day Thurber was buried, *The New Yorker* published E. B. White's warm, telling tribute to his old colleague and at times equally fractious friend. "I am one of the lucky ones," wrote White. "I knew him before blindness hit him, before fame hit him, and I tend always to think of him as a young artist in a small office in a big city, with all the world still ahead. . . . His mind was never at rest, and his pencil was connected to his mind by the best conductive tissue I have ever seen in action. The whole world knows what a funny man he was, but you had to sit next to him day after day to understand the extravagance of his clowning, the wildness and subtlety of his thinking, and the intensity of his interest in others and his sympathy for their dilemmas — dilemmas he instantly enlarged, put in focus, and made immortal, just as he enlarged and made immortal the strange goings on in the Ohio home of his boyhood." [25]

White knew that Thurber probably was best remembered for "The Secret Life of Walter Mitty," but the Thurber tale he liked even more, he wrote, was *The Last Flower*, containing as it did Thurber's "faith in the renewal of life, his feeling for the beauty and fragility of life on earth."

"And of all the flowers, real and figurative, that will find their way to Thurber's last resting place, the one that will remain fresh and wilt-proof is the little flower he himself drew, on the last page of that lovely book." [26]

Indeed, engraved on gray granite, that flower still graces Thurber's grave. His life was buffeted, his spirit sometimes bent like the blossom he drew, but his work and the laughter it continues to inspire endures as that flower does, and brightens our world.

"*All right, have it your way – you heard a seal bark!*"

"*That's my first wife up there, and this is the* present Mrs. Harris."

"What have you done with Dr. Millmoss?"

"For Heaven's sake,
why don't you go outdoors and trace something?"

"Well, if I called the wrong number, why did you answer the phone?"

"You said a moment ago that everybody you look at seems to be a rabbit.
Now just what do you mean by that, Mrs. Sprague?"

"It's a naïve domestic Burgundy without any breeding,
but I think you'll be amused by its presumption."

Destinations

A Thurber Portfolio

In 1959, a correspondent asked Thurber which of his hundreds of published cartoons he liked the best. Omitting the "too often mentioned" Seal in the Bedroom, Lady on the Bookcase, and "Touché!," he selected six others from his book *Men, Women and Dogs* that seemed to him most representative of his work.[1] Four of the six feature women in an unflattering light, and if we add The Seal in the Bedroom and The Lady on the Bookcase, six of the eight do so. One observer said Thurber's women had no sex appeal, to which Marc Connelly, the playwright and Algonquin wit, replied that they did for Thurber's men.

The men in Thurber's cartoons often are bald and stooped, sport bow ties, and wear pince-nez along with a pained or baffled expression. His women usually are dumpy, have dank, stringy hair, wear cloche hats, and are the domineering aggressors in most situations. Charles Holmes wrote that Thurber's drawings showed an undisguised hostility toward women, but Rosemary Thurber pointedly wonders what her father's drawings "do for *men*? Is there any big hero in any of them? I'm not so sure." Thurber's cartoon world is populated largely by "strong women and passive men," she notes, with sympathy not especially accorded to the "weaker" of the two.[2]

Indeed, men are not always the victims in Thurber's cartoons. In a series called "The Masculine Approach," they are depicted as manipulative cads, with their courting behavior witheringly dissected. They are shown employing wooing approaches Thurber characterized as "The You'll-Never-See-Me-Again Tactics," "The Let-'Em-Wait-And-Wonder Plan," "The Unhappy-Childhood Story," "The Just-a-Little-Boy System," and "The I'm-Not-Good-Enough-for-You Announcement." [3] In his seventeen-drawing series "The War Between Men and Women," the males — who start the fight — eventually triumph, with the female general surrendering a symbolic baseball bat to her conquering counterpart. That ceremony may have signaled more of a cease-fire, however, than an actual surrender, Thurber noted. He advised an interviewer to observe that "each woman has a big rock or club behind her back," indicating that "the war is not over, so far as she's concerned." [4]

In Thurber's favorite cartoons, the women are not the surrendering type. The wife in The Seal in the Bedroom clearly has little patience with her baffled spouse's insistence that he has heard a seal bark. Dorothy Parker wondered what happened *before* the seal found its way behind the headboard of that bed, but perhaps an even greater subject for bemused speculation is what happened a few moments *after* the scene we see, when perhaps the wife heard a flipper flap, or looked up and saw the seal. As curious as we may be about how the seal silently stole into the bedroom, imagine the uproar when it tried to get out. The drawing in this cartoon is typically sketchy — the husband's hand looks like a seal flipper itself — but, as usual, the idea is the thing. Thurber proudly recalled that Robert Benchley sent him a telegram saying, "Thank you for the funniest drawing caption ever to appear in any magazine!" [5] It is the caption, and the concept, that enchant us.

The origin of The Lady on the Bookcase was as accidental as The Seal in the Bedroom, Thurber said. He claimed to have intended to draw a woman crouching at the top of a stairway, but his inept attempt at drawing the stairs led to their transformation into a bookcase, and thence to the curious scene that confronts us. The editors at *The New*

Yorker wanted to know if the woman atop the bookcase was alive or dead, and if deceased, whether she was stuffed for display. Thurber said she was alive, but when Ross asked why she was lurking in such a spot, Thurber replied, "You have me there, Ross, I'm not responsible for the behavior of my characters." * 6

Dorothy Parker was among those puzzled by the genus and species of "that strange beast" that stands beside a pipe, shoe, and hat, and gazes enigmatically at the woman who, arms akimbo, demands to know, "What have you done with Dr. Millmoss?" Thurber identified the beast as a hippopotamus, which he had drawn for his tiny daughter. "Something about the creature's expression when he was completed convinced me that he had recently eaten a man," Thurber wrote. "I added the hat and pipe and Mrs. Millmoss, and the caption followed easily enough." He said Rosemary, then two years old, had immediately identified the beast. "That's a hippotomanus," she said when shown the drawing. "*The New Yorker* was not so smart," Thurber recalled. "They described the drawing for their files as follows: 'Woman with strange beast.' *The New Yorker* was nine years old at the time." 8

Thurber said the origin of his famous dog, being hectored to "go outdoors and trace something" in a cartoon that was also one of Helen Thurber's favorites, was to be found partly in the print of the Duke of Westminster's six hunting hounds that hung in his Grandfather Fisher's home, and partly in the constraints placed upon his drawings of them

*Dr. John Halperin, Centennial Professor of English at Vanderbilt University, suggests that in The Lady on the Bookcase, Thurber was referring, consciously or unconsciously, to the opening lines of "My Last Duchess," a Robert Browning poem Thurber certainly knew: "That's my last Duchess painted on the wall/Looking as if she were alive." The reader infers from the poem that the Duke had done her in. Who's to say whether Thurber intended to plant the reference? But given his fondness for twisting literary allusions, it is a reasonable supposition.7

when he visited the office of a businessman friend in Columbus and pestered him by doodling dogs on every page of his note pads. Unable to fit a completed bloodhound on the tiny note pad paper, Thurber appended the stubby legs of a basset hound to the large head of a brooding, thoughtful bloodhound and thereby devised his own special breed. He wrote that his dogs, like those in his grandfather's lithograph, have "dignity and common sense, two qualities which the people I draw are said not to possess." [9]

A strain certainly was placed upon the dignity and common sense of the Thurber dog belonging to the irritated and irrational lady who demands of the person on the other end of her telephone line, "Well, if I called the wrong number, why did you answer the phone?" The ears of the dog are raised in astonishment, and the lady's husband, sitting nearby, is similarly perplexed. Rosemary Thurber says that her father "told me once that it was my mother who gave him that caption," although he never made clear "whether she gave it to him from having said that and done it," adding with a laugh, "I've had momentary, total lapses like that. . . . To me, the woman in that cartoon looks like my mother. She had short, dark hair at that time. But she was not stupid, so she may just have . . . thought it up." [10]

Thurber told a British reporter in 1961 that this drawing was a fine example of "the stupidity of our species" and seemed "typical of the female intelligence." [11] Whenever he tried to deny his misogyny, he was not particularly convincing.

Something akin to sympathy for a lady in distress can be seen, however, in the cartoon dealing with the strange affliction of Mrs. Sprague, to whom everyone seems to be a rabbit – including the bow-tied, pince-nezed but definitely long-eared doctor she has gone to consult. The terror in her expression is arresting. In many of Thurber's drawings one finds, as Charles Holmes observed, "a touch of that strange, dreamlike quality which was always to be one of the hallmarks of Thurber's imagination." [12] It is dreamlike, yes; and sometimes nightmarish, too.

Nothing strange or dreamlike is depicted around the dinner table of the budding oenophile who touts the vin ordinaire in the raised glasses of his guests by saying: "It's a naïve domestic Burgundy without any breeding, but I think you'll be amused by its presumption." As a satire on the pretentiousness of many a would-be wine connoisseur, it is as sharp, accurate, and funny today as it was a half-century ago. The bug-eyed enthusiasm of the host, the adoring gaze of his supportive spouse, and the nearly blank yet quizzical look on the faces of their friends are splendid examples of Thurber's ability to convey subtle expressions with the simplest of lines.

More complex in appearance, and ironically dark in meaning, is Thurber's scene of purposeful pedestrians scurrying past a cemetery, all intent on their immediate goals and oblivious to their ultimate "Destinations." No one is spared. The little boy and scampering dog will end up beneath the sod, too, along with the top-hatted plutocrat, lunchbox-toting worker, fashionably dressed ladies, harried business-man, and cloth-capped youth. While some of their paths may be glory-bound, all will lead to the grave. Truth was the foundation for all of Thurber's humor.

8

The Old Word Man

On a Sunday morning in the fall of 1991, less than a week before the thirtieth anniversary of his death, the eleven-year-old daughter of a Los Angeles couple heard a friend of her parents refer to James Thurber.

"Oh," said the girl, "he wrote *The 13 Clocks*."

That is part of the Thurber legacy.

A few months earlier, a sixty-eight-year-old African-American, a retired postal service supervisor, saw a fellow exerciser at a health club in downtown Baltimore reading a Thurber book while pedaling on a stationery bicycle. Pointing to the volume, the older man said, "I used to love all of his stuff."

That, too, is part of the legacy of James Thurber.

At 77 Jefferson Avenue in Columbus, Ohio, hundreds of visitors a year, many from other countries, come to walk through the three-story, red brick house in which the bed supposedly fell one night on Thurber's father. A six-foot-high bronze statue of a unicorn now graces an adjacent park, surrounded in season by lilies.

Those who have come to the Thurber House in recent years include Russell Baker, *The New York Times* columnist; Garrison Keillor, the radio storyteller and essayist, now also a *New Yorker* contributor, whose mythical Midwestern enclave, Lake Wobegon, is home to folks who surely would have felt comfortable in the semimythical Columbus of Thurber's youth; and John Updike, the novelist, essayist and poet.

All came to pay homage to Thurber and to say what his legacy meant to them.

Baker called the semifictional *My Life and Hard Times* "possibly the shortest and most elegant autobiography ever written," adding that modern biographers, historians, and autobiographers, particularly politicians and their amanuenses, would do well to emulate Thurber's brevity. Baker said Thurber's comic essays are "jewels of English writing," and observed that the preservation of the Thurber House, rescued from bulldozers in the early 1980s, "suggests that despite talk about our galloping illiteracy Americans can still be hospitable to the English language when it is used with loving care." Thurber's mother, shouting a warning to her sons from that house as they got into the family car — "Now don't you dare drive all over town without gasoline!" — had earned herself "a place alongside Captain Ahab, Daisy Miller, Ma Joad, and all those others who go on and on," Baker said.[1]

Keillor often cites the influence of E. B. White on his humorous writing, but he clearly owes as deep a debt to Thurber, *Baltimore Sun* critic Tim Warren has noted. In Keillor's 1993 anthology, *The Book of Guys,* the "Whimsical, often melancholic, musings about men and women . . . are straight out of Thurber Country," Warren has written. Keillor's pieces about "aggressive women, passive-aggressive and persecuted men" all "draw directly" on Thurber's work.[2]

Updike recalled that Thurber had been the idol of his adolescence and had caused him to hoard pennies in order to buy the latest Thurber anthology, or else ask to be given it for Christmas. In 1944 or 1945, at the age of twelve or thirteen, he even sent Thurber a fan letter and received a drawing in reply — a treasure he framed and has taken with him everywhere since and still keeps not ten feet from his writing desk.[3] When *The New York Times* asked Updike what book most influenced his decision to become a writer, he replied by citing Thurber's *Men,*

Women and Dogs, a 1943 volume that remains "bathed in a numinous glow" in his memory. Albeit a collection of cartoons, it "spoke to me of New York, of sophistication, of amusing adult misery, of carefree creativity (I could see that Thurber had a lot of trouble fitting his furniture around his people but hadn't let it bother him), of nervous squiggles given permanence and celebrity by the intervening miracle of printer's ink. This struck me as a super way to live, to be behind such a book."[4] So had it not been for Mrs. Sprague, to whom everyone looked like a rabbit, perhaps there would have been no trilogy on Harry "Rabbit" Angstrom, or any of Updike's other acclaimed works.

Middle-aged adults who were children when Thurber was in his prime, and those, like the eleven-year-old girl in California, who are children now, are not the only ones for whom Thurber has significance. Today's college students also know his work, Updike notes. "In this day of fast turnover," he says, "that's pretty good."[5]

In the view of the Canadian scholar Stephen A. Black, Thurber "defines the comedy of the present age." His work "is the primary transmission line between the 'native American humor' of the nineteenth century," as embodied by Mark Twain, and "the tragicomic fiction of such writers as Salinger, Bellow, Roth, Malamud, Heller" and others. Thurber was also, in Black's opinion, "almost the only comic writer of his generation whose fiction has consistent literary excellence."[6]

Toward the end of his life, Thurber wanted above all to be taken seriously. "I try to make as perceptive and helpful comment on the human predicament as I can, in fables, fairy tales, stories, and essays," he wrote. "I am surprised that so few people see the figure of seriousness in the carpet of my humor and comedy." To a British interviewer he complained bitterly in February 1961, "I have written as many savage pieces as humorous ones. How many years will it take to convince people I'm not a clown?"[7]

In calmer moments, Thurber knew that humor could be powerful, and that those who created it wielded just as potent a weapon as any serious or "savage" writer. "Humor is as big a fist as any other form, or maybe bigger," he wrote to E. B. White in 1951; it is the "only solvent of terror and tension," as he put it in *Lanterns and Lances* a decade later.[8]

In the early 1930s, Thurber had defined humor for Max Eastman as "a kind of emotional chaos told about calmly and quietly in retrospect." The best humor, he said, "lies closest to the familiar, distressing, even tragic," and the chortles it provokes are akin to "that hysterical laugh that people sometimes get in the face of the Awful."[9] With tongue only slightly in cheek, he wrote in the introduction to *My Life and Hard Times* that comedy had somber origins; that humorists were more aware of the everyday woes that afflict their compatriots than of those larger dangers imperiling the nation and the world — although they may be vaguely aware of those, too. The work of humorists, while it might amuse the reader, does not spring from a sense of frivolity or joy, Thurber wrote, but rather from darker, sadder impulses deep within the writers. "The little wheels of their invention are set in motion by the damp hand of melancholy."[10]

As Catherine McGehee Kenney has observed, Dostoyevsky and Kierkegaard both recognized that comedy and tragedy are inextricably related, as are laughter and tears, hope and despair, order and chaos. These pairings represent the "extremes of human experience" that "touch in terrible tension," and it is such a tension "that gives Thurber's art its enduring brilliance, interest and energy."[11]

Thurber's humor usually inspires a grin or chuckle, not a guffaw. As he aged, Thurber worried about that as well. In a piece written just prior to the Broadway opening of *A Thurber Carnival*, in February 1960, he fretted that modern theatergoers seemed to demand "the wow, the yak, the belly-laugh," as opposed to something that evokes "the appreciative smile."[12] Yet the humor that inspires the gentle grin is the humor of personal recognition. We smile at it because we see ourselves in the people who populate the stories and the situations that envelop and, more often than not, defeat them. For Thurber, comedy reached its peak when reality became muddled, communications collapsed, confusion sprouted, and whatever was going on began spinning out of control. Humor that is based on the immutable foibles of human nature is as enduring and telling as anything that elicits what Thurber scorned as "the roll-'em-in-the-aisles gagerissimo."

For Thurber, the finest art form was neither comedy nor tragedy but tragicomedy. "The true balance of life and art, the saving of the human mind as well as the theatre, lies in what has long been known as tragicomedy," he wrote, "for humor and pathos, tears and laughter are, in the highest expression of the human character and achievement, inseparable."[13] Tragicomedy for Thurber was not a hybrid featuring comic elements grafted onto tragic ones, but rather something in which the chief characters, actions, and themes are both comic and tragic at the same time.

Toward the end of his life Thurber took to denouncing what he considered the attempt by "everybody in the United States . . . to escape from reality,"[14] but in many of his best works he had celebrated the beneficial effects of fantasy. The eccentric who resists society's regimentation is Thurber's hero. "In a triumphant daydream it seems to me, there is felicity and not defeat," he wrote in *Let Your Mind Alone!* In *My Life and Hard Times,* in "Walter Mitty," fantasies and daydreams overcome the harsh blows inflicted by reality and allow the dreamers to triumph, if only in their minds. Typically, however, Thurber also acknowledged a dark side to fantasy. It was not always a sanctuary for the soul; sometimes it served as an exterminator. In "The Whip-poor-will," "A Friend to Alexander," and other stories, fantasy kills. And Mitty's final daydream is of his own execution.

Even when he championed fantasy, Thurber always insisted that his humor was founded on reality. Real, live people were the models for characters such as Barney Haller in "The Black Magic of Barney Haller" and Della in "What Do You Mean It *Was* Brillig?" Their unwitting twists of the English language transform the workaday world into a realm of the surreal. His humor, Thurber once said, was based on truth "slightly distorted for emphasis and amusement." [15]

Many readers today might not be amused by the dialectal tricks Thurber used to put a humorous spin on reality. As far back as the 1930s, some critics called for an end to dialect or ethnic humor, but Thurber vehemently defended it. A few humor writers still do. "The problem with humor today is that you don't hear any," complains Tony Kornheiser, a columnist for *The Washington Post*. "Oh, there are good jokes. But people are afraid to tell them for fear of offending somebody. Well, sure it might offend somebody. All humor is based on offending somebody. If you want to be funny and don't want to offend anybody, don't tell jokes, dress like Clarabell and carry a seltzer bottle." [16]

In his stories, at least, Thurber used dialect not to demean the subject but to open a doorway into a world of fantastic word play. Lewis Carroll would have understood Della perfectly, Thurber wrote in "What Do You Mean It *Was* Brillig?" That, for Thurber, was the highest praise.

Thurber also praised the American woman as he set about attacking her relentlessly. "I consider the American Woman the greatest potential power in the world," he said, "and altogether too complacent and lazy to do anything about it." He insisted that he was not antifeminist and even said he longed for a matriarchy. Man, he said, "had failed to run the world", so "woman must take over if the species is to survive." [17]

"Somebody has said that Woman's place is in the wrong. That's fine,"

Thurber said late in life. "What the wrong needs is a woman's presence and a woman's touch. She is far better equipped than men to set it right. The condescending male, in his pride of strength, likes to think of the female as being 'soft, soft as snow,' but just wait till he gets hit by a snowball. Almost any century now Woman may lose her patience with black politicians and red war and let fly. I wish I could be on earth to witness the saving of our self-destructive species by its greatest creative force. If I have sometimes seemed to make fun of Woman, I assure you it has only been for the purpose of egging her on." [18] Indeed, it can be argued that the women Thurber criticized the most – the overbearing Mrs. Mitty or the insufferable Ulgine Barrows – exhibited the worst attributes traditionally ascribed to men: aggressiveness, anger, domination. In his cartoon parables "The Race of Life" and *The Last Flower,* it is the women who nurture regeneration and support the faltering men.

"The only reason I draw women as savage is that they've failed to come up to the level I think they can reach," Thurber told an interviewer in 1949.[19] In 1961, however, in an unsubtle allusion to his ineffectual father, Thurber told another interviewer that America had long been the matriarchy he supposedly craved. He had recognized it as such even when he was a child. "It became obvious to me from the time I was a little boy that the American woman was in charge. . . . I think it's one of the weaknesses of America, the great dominance of the American woman." In one breath he complained about "Momism," how "the mother dominates her son," and in another he praised his own mother as "a great person," the one to whom he owed his comic sensibility.[20]

Thurber was, to put it mildly, inconsistent. He was prone to making grand pronouncements his wife Helen would dub "Jim's Friday Opinion," then completely reversing his viewpoint by Monday morning. As Lewis Gannett observed, Thurber seemed to hate mankind while liking almost everyone he ever met – "except when he is engaged in cursing his dearest friends." Thurber sardonically observed of himself: "Intelligent persons are expected to formulate 'an integrated and consistent attitude toward life or reality;' this is known as 'philosophy.' . . . Unfortunately, I have never been able to maintain a consistent attitude toward life or reality or anything else."[21] On a couple of points he appears to have maintained an unchangeable view: the superiority of animals to people, and the perils of technology. He said that anyone who looked at one of his drawings featuring a dog "should be able to see the dogs play the part of intelligence and repose."[22] He even liked to say in later years that "it would be fine if the French poodle could take over the world because they've certainly been more intelligent in the last few years than the human being, and they have great charm, grace, [and] humor." The dogs in Thurber's drawings are as victimized by women as are the men, and seem to be at one with them; a man and a hound actually waltz with each other in one cartoon, to the contemptuous disapproval of a woman, who asks: "Will you be good enough to dance this outside?"[23]

While Thurber enjoyed employing pseudotechnological jargon to comic effect, he worried that science and technology would only add to life's confusion and ultimately destroy humanity. In contrast to the then-popular view of the inevitable enhancement of life by scientific and technological advances, Thurber, like many artists before him, feared them. He took umbrage at "a world made up of gadgets that whir and whine and whiz and shriek and sometimes explode," and in *The Last Flower,* as well as in private musings, Thurber foresaw civilization's destruction by technology long before the advent of the atomic bomb made his fears seem prescient.[24] In a 1943 letter to E. B. White, he conjured up some globe-shattering weapons that were waiting in the wings for World War III even as World War II raged and, unknown to him and most of the rest of the world, the atom bomb was two years away from completion. Thurber warned White, secure on his farm up in Maine, to beware of the Mok-Mok, four of which could destroy the entire United States, and of the KM10, the Zu58, and the soaring Zo-Zo-40, which would descend upon its victims in silence. It would be unnerving for residents of Maine to know that they can be killed by something exploding in Michigan, he wrote.[25]

In many ways, Thurber was a romantic who preferred spontaneity and nature to anything formal, manufactured, or scientific. "Scientists don't really know anything about anything," he propounded as Thurber's Law in *Let Your Mind Alone!* He later scoffed at scientists "who look beyond the little menaces of the mundane moment" and remain cheerful despite these "minute portents" of civilization's degeneration.[26] He knew life to be complicated, confusing, and harsh. He thought science was incapable of addressing the basic problems of human interaction, and he believed that writers should address the concerns that individuals face in coping with life's difficulties rather than engage in political or religious theorizing. "Our everyday lives become, right after college, as unworkable as a Ford in a vat of molasses," he wrote to White in 1938, and he felt writers who were preoccupied with politics overlooked the intimate, personal woes that most affect the individual. These were the subjects to which writers should apply their art, Thurber thought. "I ought to figure but slightly in the history of humor on the barricades," he wrote to Malcolm Cowley in 1952. Thurber also was skeptical about the power of religion to soothe the troubled soul. "Man . . . is surely further away from the Answer than any other animal this side of the ladybug," he wrote in 1939.[27]

Among the early literary influences on Thurber were O. Henry, a romantic sort of figure in the history of Columbus, Ohio, having written several of his seriocomic tales there when he was doing time for embezzlement in the Ohio State Penitentiary, comic strips, whose pointed parodies of family life Thurber thoroughly enjoyed, and Western dime novels. He liked to recall having once collected, annotated, and translated "a series of dime novels, written in French, published in Paris, and devoted to the exploits of Wild Bill Hickok and his friend Buffalo Bill, who whenever he was nonplussed, exclaimed, in English, 'Mercy me!' " [28]

What occurs when romanticism confronts reality – or helps an individual overcome it – is a central feature of Thurber's comic vision. His own ideal fictional figures were the artistically and emotionally subtle gentlemen created by Henry James, and the stoic, romantic adventurers of Joseph Conrad. In the sensitive male protagonists of "the great god James," as Thurber called him, can be found the forebears of Thurber's jumpy, middle-aged men. He loved to milk the comic possibilities inherent in the conflict between the subtle world as James envisioned it and the world as it actually is; and Thurber found the stoical heroes in Conrad's fiction were the perfect models for his fictional daydreamers to idolize. [29]

To these literary tastes Thurber added a passion for the dreamlike fantasy and nonsense of Lewis Carroll, along with a strong preference for brevity and concision. He told an interviewer in 1940, "I like the perfectly done, the well-ordered, as against the sprawling chunk of life." [30] He disliked the rambling works of writers such as Thomas Wolfe, and deeply resented being dismissed once by Wolfe at a cocktail party as someone whose work was inconsequential because it was short. F. Scott Fitzgerald, whom Thurber admired, had told Wolfe, "You're a putter-inner and I'm a taker-outer," and Thurber enjoyed quoting that exchange while approving of Fitzgerald's philosophy. He told George Plimpton and Max Steele in 1958 that he had never wanted to write a long work, and that most of the books he liked best were brief: *The Great Gatsby, The Turn of the Screw, The Red Badge of Courage,* and Conrad's short stories.[31]

Thurber also recognized his own limitations. He knew that his mind turned instinctively toward the comic, and that by inclination and training he was ill-suited for long works. In 1931, he wrote to a friend that he didn't think he could produce a long, serious novel. "It would slowly begin to kid itself, and God knows what it would turn out to be like."[32] A few years later, he wrote to John McNulty that all of his years of writing short pieces for *The New Yorker* had permanently shaped his style. "I find most of my stories, after I have typed them, run to 6 and a half or seven pages. I haven't tried for that. My brain has unconsciously formed that kind of mould for them. In a way this is bad, because everything I start – play, two-volume novel, or what-not, finally rounds itself out into 6 or 7 pages – seems complete, too."[33]

Simplicity – at least in appearance – is also the hallmark of Thurber's cartoons. He turned the barest of graphic skills into a sophisticated means of artistic expression. The men in Thurber's drawings are all "given to bewilderment, vacillation, uncertainty, and downright fear," he wrote to a friend, and the women are either overpowering and bossy or infuriatingly vapid. One British art critic said of Thurber's women: "Inside every Little Nell there lurks a Lady MacBeth."[34] Many of the situations and images in Thurber's cartoons seem to have sprung spontaneously from the recesses of his subconscious. He enjoyed referring to himself as a Pre-Intentionalist, claiming that often he just started to draw "while . . . thinking of something else," let the doodle suggest a situation, then "stumbled onto the caption as easily and unexpectedly as the seal had stumbled into the bedroom." His cartoon creations, he wrote, were as "simple or, if you like, as complicated as that."[35]

Dorothy Parker, in her introduction to *The Seal in the Bedroom,* observed that Thurber's drawings always depict "culminations. Beneath his pictures he sets only the final line. You may figure for yourself, and good luck to you, what under heaven could have gone before, that his somber citizens find themselves in such remarkable situations. It is yours to ponder how penguins get into drawing rooms and seals into bed-chambers, for Mr. Thurber will only show them to you some little time after they have arrived there. . . . He gives you a glimpse of the startling present and lets you construct the astounding past." [36]

Thurber believed that the best of his cartoons were those that were the product of accident or the subconscious. When he started out with the caption first and then tried to draw something intentionally, he told an interviewer, "a stiffness was likely to get into the figures . . . and then the fact that I am not a draftsman — never took a lesson — can't really draw — came out." [37] Ironically, one of Thurber's most famous cartoons, and one in which the line is wonderfully fluid and adept, came from someone else's idea. The drawing of two fencers in which one has sliced off the head of his startled opponent and briskly proclaimed "Touché!" actually was based on a drawing originally done by another *New Yorker* cartoonist, Carl Rose. Rose was an excellent draftsman, and *The New Yorker*'s editors felt his rendition of the fencers was a little too grisly to be funny. It was proposed that Thurber do the cartoon instead, since the figures he drew were surreal to begin with, and readers would not think that any decapitated man Thurber drew was dead, but only mildly inconvenienced. [38]

Thurber's drawings are the purest expressions of his creativity, and they tend to echo in our memories like the subconscious thoughts from which they came. Their chief merit, Thurber observed, was that they were, and are, funny. "And that's what they were intended to be," he said. "They weren't intended to be a special form of art over which I struggled. Because I don't think any drawing ever took me more than three minutes." In fact, Thurber wrote to a friend, his best stuff was drawn "with pencil while cockeyed." Sometimes the humor in them is lighthearted; occasionally it is satiric; more often, it is laced with worry and fear.[39]

Of fears and anxieties, Thurber had more than a full measure, and it is a tribute to his tenacity and courage that the scope of his artistic vision expanded even as his eyesight failed. "A blind writer does not have the distractions of the writer who can see," Thurber told Alistair Cooke with pardonable bravado. "I can sit in a room and I don't look out the window; I don't become distracted by flying birds or the breeze or a pretty girl walking by. Of course I can still *hear* a pretty girl." To a reporter from *Newsweek,* Thurber revealed a touch of his stern, Midwestern belief that difficulties were beneficial to those who overcome them. "What a writer needs is handicaps," he said.[40]

It is remarkable, but perhaps not surprising, that among Thurber's initial reactions to the loss of his sight was the creation of works unlike any he had done before – fairy tales. These stories, critic Edmund Wilson wrote, signaled Thurber's "rapid elimination of the last vestiges of the conventional humorist and his emergence as a comic artist of the top layer of our contemporary writing."[41] Thurber retreated into a world of children's fantasy and reaffirmed the ideals of late-nineteenth-century Romanticism that formed the core of his artistic and personal tastes, and which were of even greater importance to him when his own creative and mental future was precarious. As Richard Tobias and Charles S. Holmes have noted, in each of Thurber's fairy tales, *Many Moons* (1943), *The Great Quillow* (1944), *The White Deer* (1945), *The 13 Clocks* (1950), and *The Wonderful O* (1957), it is the artist empowered by love – the jester, toymaker, poetic younger son, minstrel-prince, or poet – who saves the day. The supposed wise men – the royal advisers, scientists, attorneys, accountants, and wizards – are unable to solve the conundrums or conquer the villains. Thurber also used the fairy tales to address a theme that remained constant throughout all of his works: the ambiguous, perpetually shifting nature of reality as we perceive it.[42]

E. B. White wrote to Thurber that *The White Deer* was "Exhibit A in the strange case of a writer's switch from eye work to ear work"; he generously marveled that "anybody could make such a switch and live."[43] The writing style in all of the fairy tales is distinct from Thurber's essays and stories. It is an almost baroque combination of poetry and prose, a graceful blending of alliteration, internal rhyme, and meticulously crafted rhythm. His visual impairment did not hamper his growth as an artist.

Most of the humor in the fairy tales comes from wordplay, and language, always the chief subject of fascination for Thurber, gradually became an obsession. When language was ill-used, the culture was imperiled. He saw language as providing "both a possibility of achieving the most precise balance in a chaotic world," and a vehicle likely to spark chaos, Kenney observed. Thurber's "greatest contribution to life and letters is his passionate devotion to discovering sense in a world of nonsense." His humor, she contends, "is the supreme balancing act of a humorist who was really a poet, of an artist who attempted to see life steadily and whole while the universe was turning madly about him."[44]

A decline in the use of the English language was just one of the subjects Thurber groused about in his later pieces, many of which assumed an aggressively pedantic tone. Instead of the inept, retiring, essentially tolerant and appealing Thurber who appears in his earlier essays and stories, the Thurber of the 1950s is constantly engaging lesser intellects in cocktail or dinner party conversations and defeating them with barrages of puns and literary allusions. His condescension and vanity seem palpable, and the change in his comic persona is not especially attractive. An air of desperation also pervades many of these pieces. The bumbling, endearing, neurotic Thurber of the 1930s now is an equally neurotic but defiant drinker and sufferer from insomnia who compulsively dissects words, phrases, and famous literary quotations, moves the pieces around, and fights to demonstrate his intellectual superiority. Unlike the artful, concise smoothness of Thurber's best works, crafted like the paragraphs of his idol Robert O. Ryder to make the meticulously wrought seem effortless, many of the later pieces often are rambling and strained. In them, John Updike observed sadly in a review of *Credos and Curios,* the first posthumously published collection of Thurber's later pieces, "logomachic tricks are asked to pass for wit and implausible pun-swapping for human conversation."[45]

Although Thurber had always viewed life as a constant state of confusion bordering on chaos, his finest works contain what Kenney calls a "coupling of savage disillusionment and realistic hope that gives enduring value and richness to Thurber's best treatments of the human predicament." In his later work, hope seems to have fled. Thurber was dismayed by what he considered the decline in practically everything, and his annoyance was "so inclusive as to be pointless," Updike wrote. "The writer who had produced 'Fables for Our Time' and 'The Last Flower' out of the thirties had become, by the end of the fifties, one more indignant senior citizen penning complaints about the universal decay of virtue."[46]

Yet while much of Thurber's later writing seems unrelievedly grumpy and misanthropic, it also has moments of prescience, as did his earlier work. Some of the symptoms of cultural decline that he diagnosed more than thirty years ago are pervasive now. In 1961, he grumbled that "it is becoming harder and harder, in our time, to tell government from show business"; a few years earlier, he complained about the "craving of television audiences for blood and brutality," and "the crumbling of precision and sense" in English usage.[47]

Few subjects caused Thurber to fret more than the health of humor, which he found in parlous condition. In written discourses and dozens of interviews he deplored the state of humor in the "jumpy" and "jittery" postwar world, and he wondered bleakly whether any new humorists would come along to resuscitate comedy. Toward the end of his life, however, he reported cheering "signs of . . . [a] coming revival, for humor is innate and resilient."[48] He was ecstatic about the advent of Art Buchwald, whose work he praised in a generous, open fan letter to *The New York Times* in April 1959: "Art Buchwald, a prominent nonconformist, insists on being funny in the good old-fashioned way — that is, amusing, entertaining, and hilarious."[49] At the time Thurber wrote that letter, Russell Baker still was a daily political reporter for the *Times,* Erma Bombeck was a harried young housewife, and Woody Allen was writing television sketches for Sid Caesar. Had Thurber lived to see their best work, his fears for humor's future might have been alleviated.

In assuming the role of a nearly perpetual pallbearer for comedy, Thurber perhaps was unconsciously acknowledging that his own sense of humor was seriously ill, and his ability to create humor had gone. "You have to enjoy humorous writing while you're doing it," he had told Max Eastman in 1936. "You can't be mad, or bitter, or irate. If you are it will be no good." Now he was mad, bitter and irate most of the time, and his writing showed it. He remarked ruefully to George Plimpton and Max Steele in 1958 that there seemed to be a "curious idea that the writer's inventiveness and ability will end in his fifties." Keats had worried that he would die before his pen had "glean'd . . . [his] teeming brain," Thurber said, whereas an American writer was "more likely to fear that his brain may cease to teem." His own brain still teemed, Thurber assured his interviewers confidently, even defiantly. Regrettably, few sparks now were struck from all his cerebral activity.[50]

There is irony in the fact that many of Thurber's later works – the ones written closer to our own time – age less well than those he wrote in the 1920s and 1930s about a period even more remote than that, the years before the World War I. Thurber's earlier pieces deal with timeless human characters and situations. In the later pieces, employing his incredible memory of the literary chestnuts of his youth – and, indeed, cleverly paraphrasing and parodying them – he unwittingly dated the humor. The allusions to Longfellow, Tennyson, Browning, Wordsworth, Shelley, Emerson, and others whose works are obscure to many modern readers, unfortunate though that may be, render these pieces labored and unfunny. The best humor, Thurber had told Max Eastman, "lies closest to the familiar." By ignoring that rule and basing his later humor on sources that since have become unfamiliar, he dulled the edge of his wit.[51]

Thurber's memory and literary sensibility were used to far better advantage in the warm, perceptive tributes and memorials he wrote praising friends and colleagues. He was masterful at capturing the essence of a personality in succinct, telling anecdotes, and at balancing analysis with eulogy. Given the dismal tone in much of the later Thurber pieces reprinted in *Credos and Curios*, which was published in 1962, it is easy to share the regret Helen Thurber expressed, in her introduction to the book, about the stories she knew her husband meant to write but never managed to compose: "An Evening with Hemingway," "Shake Hands with Sinclair Lewis," and "Cocktails with Thomas Wolfe." Their titles were listed in a preliminary table of contents, scribbled in Thurber's nearly illegible scrawl, which she found among his papers after his death. And we can be even sorrier, as was Helen Thurber, who died in December 1986,[*] that her husband's written recollections of Columbus, Ohio, never included his oft-recited story of Miss Naddy's Dancing Academy, located above a bowling alley. There most of the young men carried guns, puffed on cigars, but somehow never intimidated the redoubtable Miss Naddy. "All right, now we'll try another moonlight waltz," she would bellow, "and this time I want you guys to stay out from behind them palms!" [52]

In fact, Thurber told an interviewer in 1959 that his wife had found thirty-seven unfinished articles in his files, including one piece marked "Preface to Something. Hold." Thurber remarked: "I'm thinking of using that for the title of my collected works." [53] In the introduction to *Thurber Country,* an anthology published six years earlier, Thurber had suggested that his collected works be titled "The Anatomy of Confusion," ironically juxtaposing the contrast between the chaotic events he chronicled – the battle of the sexes, garbled language, institutional and mechanical mix-ups – and the methodical manner in which he analyzed them.[54] Regardless of its title, Thurber's collected works surely would have been enhanced by his recollections and assessments of Hemingway, Lewis, and Wolfe, written in the same style as the superb tributes to E. B. White, Robert Benchley, Mary Petty, and others that are the finest pieces in *Credos and Curios.* In these appreciations, Thurber is at his best: incisive, generous, affectionate – and funny.

We all hope that the traits we most admire in others we somehow share ourselves, and in putting Thurber's personality and accomplishments in perspective it is proper to appropriate some of the judgments he passed on others and apply them to him. In Thurber's drawings one finds, as he wrote of Mary Petty's devilish, Edwardian-style cartoons

---

[*] Thurber's first wife, Althea, had died in April 1986.

for *The New Yorker,* an "alarming and hilarious world," a realm that is "peculiarly, jealously, devotedly" his own.[55] Thurber's best writing, influenced as it was by the example of E. B. White, shimmered as did White's prose with "silver and crystal sentences which had a ring like the ring of nobody else's sentences in the world."[56] As Thurber observed of Benchley's achievements, so it could be said of Thurber: he "left behind a rich legacy of humor, comedy, satire, parody, and criticism." The "heavier critics have underrated Benchley because of his 'short flight,' missing his distinguished contribution to the fine art of comic brevity," Thurber wrote. Much of the same could be said of his own work, in which the reader finds Thurber "ducking swiftly, looking closely, writing sharply."[57]

It is too facile to try placing Thurber in any particular school of humor, just as it was wrong, he said, to thus assign Benchley. As he wrote of Benchley, so it could be said of Thurber: He "stands alone, in a great, good place all his own . . . , unique, complete, and in the round."

Thurber's is a world like no other but one in which we feel familiar — albeit uncomfortably so — with its feuding men and women, dysfunctional families, infuriating machines, preposterous scientific or social theories, constant confusion often turning into chaos, and wise, patient animals; a world of pointed fables, philosophic musings, and reassuring fantasies; of satires, literary analyses, and short stories. Perhaps the ultimate artistic achievement is the creation of a unique universe, a place of distinctive characters, sensibilities, and situations, a world of one's own. Thurber created such a world — and said we were welcome to it. We remain grateful for that gift.

Notes

Introduction

1 Linda Zycherman, Stoneledge, Inc., telephone interview with author, Aug. 25, 1991; *New York Times,* Feb. 19, 1991, p.B1; Linda Kulman, publicity manager, *The New Yorker,* letter to author, Mar. 2, 1992.

2 E. B. and Katharine S. White, *A Subtreasury of American Humor,* p.vviii.

3 James Thurber, "The Lady on the Bookcase," *The Beast in Me,* p.67.

4 Thurber, "The Lady on the Bookcase," p.75.

5 Robert van Gelder, "Thurber's Life and Hard Times," *New York Times Book Review,* May 12, 1940, reprinted in Thomas Fensch, ed., *Conversations with James Thurber,* p.11.

6 George Plimpton and Max Steele, "James Thurber," from *Writers at Work: The Paris Review Interviews,* reprinted in Fensch, ed., *Conversations,* p.54.

7 Plimpton and Steele, "James Thurber," p.54.

8 Joseph Deitch, "Breakfast with Thurber," *Christian Science Monitor,* Aug. 9, 1951, reprinted in Fensch, ed., *Conversations,* p.27.

9 Russell Baker, "He Knew When to Stop," *The New York Times,* Apr. 12, 1990.

10 John Ferris, "Thurber Has His Own Brand of Humor," *The Columbus Citizen,* Nov. 8, 1953, reprinted in Fensch, ed., *Conversations,* p.35.

11 Thurber, *Alarms and Diversions,* p.66.

12 Catherine McGehee Kenney, *Thurber's Anatomy of Confusion,* pp.146–47.

13 Kenney, *Anatomy of Confusion,* pp.162–63.

14 Kenney, *Anatomy of Confusion*, p.153.

15 Kenney, *Anatomy of Confusion*, p.154.

16 John Winokur, *Writers on Writing*, p.316, cited in Douglas P. Bruns, "In the Beginning Was the Word," *The Baltimore Evening Sun*, Mar. 25, 1992.

17 Letter to Joel and Gertrude Sayer, Dec. 22, 1950, collected in Helen Thurber and Edward Weeks, eds., *The Selected Letters of James Thurber*, p.187.

18 Jonathan Yardley, "New Twist on Dickens," *The Washington Post*, July 29, 1992.

Chapter 1

1 Thurber, "Adam's Anvil," in *The Thurber Album*, p.33.

2 Thurber, "Man with a Rose," in *The Thurber Album*, pp.39–41. Burton Bernstein, *Thurber: A Biography*, p.5.

3 Thurber, "Time Exposures," "Conversation Piece," both in *The Thurber Album*, pp.14 and 61, respectively.

4 Charles S. Holmes, *The Clocks of Columbus*, p.8; Bernstein, *Thurber*, p.7.

5 Alistair Cooke, "James Thurber in Conversation with Alistair Cooke," *Atlantic*, Aug. 1956, pp.36–37; Thurber interview with Henry Brandon in *The New Republic*, May 26, 1958, collected in Fensch, ed., *Conversations*, p.93.

6 Bernstein, *Thurber*, p.7; Thurber, "Lavender with a Difference," in *The Thurber Album*, pp.139–41.

7 Bernstein, *Thurber*, p.8.

8 Thurber, "Gentleman from Indiana," in *The Thurber Album*, pp.111, 113, 124; Bernstein, *Thurber*, p.13.

9 Thurber, *The Thurber Carnival*, p.xi; Thurber, "Man with a Rose," p.41; Bernstein, *Thurber*, pp.13–15.

10 Dr. Thomas Connor, Jr., doctor of ophthalmology, Johns Hopkins Hospital, telephone interview with author, Aug. 1992.

11 Bernstein, *Thurber,* p.335.

12 Bernstein, *Thurber,* p.23.

13 Thurber, "I Went to Sullivant," in *The Middle-Aged Man on the Flying Trapeze,* p.101.

14 Holmes, *The Clocks of Columbus,* p.14.

15 Cooke, "James Thurber," p.36.

16 Bernstein, *Thurber,* p.29.

17 Bernstein, *Thurber,* p.30.

18 Bernstein, *Thurber,* pp.36–37.

19 Bernstein, *Thurber,* p.42; Holmes, *The Clocks of Columbus,* p.280.

20 Thurber, "University Days," in *The Thurber Carnival,* p.225.

21 Bernstein, *Thurber,* p.40.

22 Thurber, "University Days," p.223.

23 Letter to James Pollard, June 28, 1960, in Bernstein, *Thurber,* p.47.

24 Holmes, *The Clocks of Columbus,* p.34.

25 Letter to Edward Spencer, Nov. 11, 1950, quoted in Bernstein, *Thurber,* p.50.

26 Thurber, "Length and Shadow," in *The Thurber Album,* p.205.

27 Thurber, "Man with a Pipe," in *The Thurber Album,* p.179; Brandon interview, pp.104–5.

28 Thurber, "B.O.II.," in *The Thurber Album,* p.185; Holmes, *The Clocks of Columbus,* pp.31–32.

29 Nelson Budd, "Personal Reminiscences of James Thurber," *Ohio State University Monthly,* Jan. 1962, cited in Bernstein, *Thurber,* p.60.

30 Stephen Vincent and Rosemary Benét, "Thurber as Unmistakable as a Kangaroo," *New York Herald Tribune Book Review,* Dec. 19, 1940.

31 Bernstein, *Thurber,* pp.63–70.

Chapter 2

1 Thurber, "The First Time I Saw Paris," in *Alarms and Diversions*, p.8.

2 Thurber, "Exhibit X," in *The Beast In Me*, p.66; Bernstein, *Thurber*, pp.83, 85.

3 Bernstein, *Thurber*, p.92.

4 Letter to Elliott Nugent, Mar. 25, 1920, quoted in Bernstein, *Thurber*, p.98.

5 Thurber, "Newspaperman – Head and Shoulders," in *The Thurber Album*, p.220.

6 Letter to Harold Ross, Oct. 19, 1951, in Bernstein, *Thurber*, pp.111–12; Holmes, *The Clocks of Columbus*, p.56.

7 Bernstein, *Thurber*, pp.121, 172.

8 Rosemary Thurber, interview with author, Mar. 28, 1992.

9 Bernstein, *Thurber*, pp.119–22, 125.

10 Letter to Frank Gibney, Oct. 31, 1956, quoted in Bernstein, *Thurber*, p.130; Holmes, *The Clocks of Columbus*, p.63.

11 Holmes, *The Clocks of Columbus*, p.56; Bernstein, *Thurber*, p.132.

12 Thurber, *Thurber's Dogs*, pp.xi–xii; see Bernstein, *Thurber*, p.136.

13 Letter to E. B. White, Dec. 22, 1952, quoted in Bernstein, *Thurber*, p.138.

14 Letter to Hudson Hawley, July 27, 1954, letter to John Scott Mabon, March 16, 1946, both quoted in Bernstein, *Thurber*, p.140.

15 William L. Shirer, *Twentieth-Century Journey: The Start*, pp.216, 225.

16 Letter to Hawley, in Bernstein, p.141.

17 Thurber, letter to Hawley, p.141; Shirer, *The Start*, pp.226–27.

18 Bernstein, *Thurber*, pp.140–41.

19 Shirer, *The Start*, p.225.

20 Shirer, *The Start*, pp.231–33.

21 Thurber, "Scott in Thorns," in *Credos and Curios*, p.157.

22 Thurber, "Memoirs of a Drudge," in *The Thurber Carnival*, pp.18–19.

23 Thurber, "La Grande Ville de Plaisir," in *My World – and Welcome to It*, pp.259–74.

24 Bernstein, *Thurber*, p.142; Holmes, *The Clocks of Columbus*, pp.76–77.

25 Shirer, *The Start*, pp.270–71.

26 Bernstein, *Thurber*, p.147; "Thurber and His Humor," *Newsweek*, Feb. 4, 1957, pp.52–56.

Chapter 3

1 Holmes, *The Clocks of Columbus*, p.82.

2 Thurber, *The Years with Ross*, pp.33–34; Bernstein, *Thurber*, p.150.

3 Bernstein, *Thurber*, p.151.

4 Bernstein, *Thurber*, p.154; Robert Coates, "James Thurber," *Author's Guild Bulletin*, Dec. 1961.

5 Eddy Gilmore, " 'Call Me Jim': James Thurber Speaking," *Columbus Dispatch*, Aug. 3, 1958, collected in Fensch, ed., *Conversations*, p.50.

6 Thurber, "Memoirs of a Drudge," in *The Thurber Carnival*, p.22.

7 Holmes, *The Clocks of Columbus*, p.84.

8 Holmes, *The Clocks of Columbus*, p.86; Bernstein, *Thurber*, p.163.

9 Letter to Frank Gibney, Oct. 31, 1956, quoted in Bernstein, *Thurber*, p.164.

10 Thurber, *The Years with Ross*, pp.240–51.

11 Thurber, *The Years with Ross*, p.13.

12 Thurber, *The Years with Ross*, pp.5, 11.

13 Thurber, *The Years with Ross*, pp.118–19; Bernstein, *Thurber*, pp.160–61.

14 Thurber, *The Years with Ross*, p.15.

15 Thurber, "The Incomparable Mr. Benchley," in *Credòs and Curios*, p.149.

16 Neil A. Grauer, "I'm Fine, Just Hurting Inside," *American Heritage*, Apr.–May 1986, p.83.

17 Holmes, *Thurber: A Collection of Critical Essays*, p.22.

18 Grauer, "I'm Fine," p.84; Holmes, *Critical Essays*, pp.24–25.

19 E. B. White, "James Thurber," memorial, *New Yorker*, Nov. 11, 1961, quoted in Bernstein, *Thurber*, p.504.

20 Bernstein, *Thurber*, p.164; Holmes, *The Clocks of Columbus*, p.107.

21 William L. Shirer, interview with author, Nov. 20, 1991; Bernstein, *Thurber*, p.172.

22 Linda H. Davis, *Onward & Upward: A Biography of Katharine S. White*, p.88.

23 Holmes, *The Clocks of Columbus*, pp.167, 242.

24 Al Hirschfeld, interview with author, Sept. 14, 1991.

25 Bernstein, *Thurber*, p.172.

26 Thurber, "Mr. Monroe and the Moving Men," in *The Owl in the Attic*, pp.36–41.

27 Thurber, "Tea at Mrs. Armsby's," in *Owl in the Attic*, pp.3–7.

28 Letter to E. B. White, Dec. 22, 1952, in Bernstein, *Thurber*, p.175.

29 Thurber, "Ladies' and Gentlemen's Guide to Modern English," in *Owl in the Attic*, p.111.

30 Thurber, *The Years with Ross*, p.56.

31 Thurber, *The Years with Ross*, p.56.

32 Thurber, *The Years with Ross*, p.57.

33 E. B. White, introduction to 1950 edition of *Is Sex Necessary?*; Bernstein, *Thurber*, p.186.

34 E. B. White, foreword to *Is Sex Necessary?* (1929 edition).

35 E. B. White, introduction to *The Owl in the Attic*, p.xvi.

36 Dorothy Parker, introduction to *The Seal in the Bedroom*, reprinted in Holmes, *Critical Essays*, p.57.

37 Thurber, "Lo Hear the Gentle Bloodhounds," in *Thurber's Dogs*, p.260.

38 Hirschfeld interview.

39 Parker, introduction to *The Seal in the Bedroom*, p.57. Bernstein, *Thurber*, pp.193–94.

40 Thurber, *The Years with Ross*, p.58.

41 Thurber, *The Years with Ross*, pp.52–53.

42 Thurber, *The Thurber Carnival*, p.299.

43 Bernstein, *Thurber*, p.191.

44 Thurber, *Thurber's Dogs,* pp.221–22; Kenney, *Thurber's Anatomy of Confusion,* p.76.

45 Bernstein, *Thurber,* p.196; Thurber, *The Years with Ross,* pp.65–66.

46 Thurber, *The Years with Ross,* p.66.

47 Rosemary Thurber, interview with author, Mar. 28, 1992.

48 Rosemary Thurber interview.

49 Letter to E. B. White, Jan. 20, 1938, in Holmes, *The Clocks of Columbus,* p.187.

50 Elliott Nugent, "Notes on James Thurber, the Man, or Men," *New York Times,* Feb. 25, 1940, quoted in Holmes, *The Clocks of Columbus,* p.204.

51 Heywood Hale Broun, interview with author, Sept. 24, 1991.

52 Thurber, "One Is a Wanderer," in *The Thurber Carnival,* pp.166–68.

53 Bernstein, *Thurber,* p.218.

54 Max Eastman, *Enjoyment of Laughter,* p.342; Holmes, *The Clocks of Columbus,* pp.148–51.

55 Robert van Gelder, "Thurber's Life and Hard Times," *The New York Times Book Review,* May 12, 1940, reprinted in Fensch, ed., *Conversations,* p.12.

56 Holmes, *The Clocks of Columbus,* p.151.

57 Rosemary Thurber interview.

58 Holmes, *The Clocks of Columbus,* p.179; Bernstein, *Thurber,* pp.215–16.

59 Bernstein, *Thurber,* p.242.

60 Bernstein, *Thurber,* p.246.

61 Bernstein, *Thurber,* p.252.

62 Thurber, "A Couple of Hamburgers," in *The Thurber Carnival,* pp.93–94.

Chapter 4

1 Bernstein, *Thurber,* pp.258–59.

2 Holmes, *The Clocks of Columbus,* pp.174–75.

3 Thurber, "The Black Magic of Barney Haller," in *The Thurber Carnival,* pp.136–39.

4 Thurber, "Mr. Prebel Gets Rid of His Wife," in *The Middle-Aged Man on the Flying Trapeze*.

5 Charles Poore, *New York Times*, Nov. 24, 1935, quoted in Holmes, *The Clocks of Columbus*, p.179.

6 Bernstein, *Thurber*, pp.261–62.

7 Thurber, "Two O'Clock at the Metropole," in Robert Lopresti, ed., *Thurber on Crime*, p.69.

8 Bernstein, *Thurber*, p.263.

9 Holmes, *The Clocks of Columbus*, p.181.

10 Holmes, *The Clocks of Columbus*, p.182.

11 Bernstein, *Thurber*, p.270.

12 Holmes, *The Clocks of Columbus*, p.180.

13 Letter to Herman Miller, Oct. 1936, quoted in Bernstein, *Thurber*, p.275.

14 Thurber, "The Admiral on the Wheel," in *The Thurber Carnival*, pp.90–91.

15 Bernstein, *Thurber*, p.177.

16 Thurber, "Voices of Resolution," *The New Republic*, Mar. 25, 1936, quoted in Holmes, *The Clocks of Columbus*, p.193.

17 Bernstein, *Thurber*, p.279.

18 *The Daily Sketch*, London, May 25, 1937, quoted in Holmes, *The Clocks of Columbus*, p.183.

19 Bernstein, *Thurber*, p.280.

20 Holmes, *The Clocks of Columbus*, p.184.

21 Thurber, "There's No Place Like Home," in *My World – and Welcome to It*, pp.303–4.

22 Bernstein, *Thurber*, p.298.

23 Thurber, *My World - and Welcome to It*, p.211.

24 Bernstein, *Thurber*, pp.302–3.

25 Thurber, "What Do You Mean It *Was* Brillig?" in *The Thurber Carnival*, pp.43–46.

26 Kenney, *Thurber's Anatomy of Confusion*, p.97; Bernstein, *Thurber*, p.307.

27 The tales were originally collected in *Fables for Our Time and Famous Poems Illustrated*, then anthologized in *The Thurber Carnival*, pp.245–68.

28 Kenney, *Anatomy of Confusion*, pp.102–3.

29 Holmes, *The Clocks of Columbus*, p.214.

30 Bernstein, *Thurber*, pp.310–11.

31 Thurber, "The Secret Life of Walter Mitty," in *The Thurber Carnival*, p.47.

32 Bernstein, *Thurber*, p.254.

33 Cooke, "James Thurber in Conversation with Alistair Cooke," *Atlantic*, Aug. 1956, pp.36–37; Bernstein, *Thurber*, p.311.

34 Bernstein, *Thurber*, p.312.

35 Holmes, *The Clocks of Columbus*, p.216.

36 Bernstein, *Thurber*, p.391; "Two Communications: Goldwyn vs. Thurber," *Life*, Aug. 4, 1947.

37 Letter to Mrs. Robert Blake, Apr. 7, 1961, quoted in Bernstein, *Thurber*, p.311.

38 Holmes, *The Clocks of Columbus*, p.189.

39 Thurber, "Roaming in the Gloaming," *New York Times*, 1940, quoted in Holmes, *The Clocks of Columbus*, pp.202–3.

40 Bernstein, *Thurber*, pp.317–18.

41 Bernstein, *Thurber*, pp.267, 380–81.

42 Bernstein, *Thurber*, p.318.

43 W. H. Auden, "The Icon and the Portrait," *The Nation*, Jan. 13, 1940, p.48.

44 Kenney, *Anatomy of Confusion*, p.141.

45 Letter to E. B. White, Nov. 1939, quoted in Bernstein, *Thurber*, p.321.

46 Bernstein, *Thurber*, p.327.

47 Letter to Herman and Dorothy Miller, Mar. 19, 1940, quoted in Bernstein, *Thurber*, p.328.

48 Letter to Dr. Gordon Bruce, June 9, 1939, quoted in Bernstein, *Thurber,* p.314.

Chapter 5

1 Letter to Dr. Gordon Bruce, spring 1940, quoted in Bernstein, *Thurber,* p.330.

2 Thurber, "You Could Look It Up," in *My World - and Welcome to It,* p.106; "Midget Story Gets New Twist by Veeck," *The Sporting News,* Aug. 29, 1951; Holmes, *The Clocks of Columbus,* pp.219, 222.

3 Holmes, *The Clocks of Columbus,* p.215.

4 Thurber, "If You Ask Me," *PM,* Sept. 19, 1940, quoted in Holmes, *The Clocks of Columbus,* p.215.

5 Bernstein, *Thurber,* p.334.

6 Letter to Ronald and Jane Williams, May 1941, quoted in Bernstein, *Thurber,* p.336.

7 Holmes, *The Clocks of Columbus,* pp.224, 230.

8 Bernstein, *Thurber,* p.340.

9 Thurber, "The Whip-Poor-Will," in *My World – and Welcome to It,* p.31; "A Friend to Alexander," in *My World,* p.153.

10 Bernstein, *Thurber,* p.338.

11 Letter to Dr. Gordon Bruce, Aug. 1941, quoted in Bernstein, *Thurber,* p.341.

12 Bernstein, *Thurber,* p.341.

13 Bernstein, *Thurber,* pp.344–51.

14 Letter to Frank Gibney, Oct. 31, 1956, quoted in Bernstein, *Thurber,* pp.344–45.

15 Bernstein, *Thurber,* pp.343–44.

16 Unsent letter to Ernest Hemingway, Jan. 11, 1961, quoted in Bernstein, *Thurber,* pp.482–83.

17 Bernstein, *Thurber,* p.349.

18 Stephen A. Black, *James Thurber: His Masquerades*, p.23; see also Holmes, *The Clocks of Columbus*, p.216.

19 Bernstein, *Thurber*, p.350; Holmes, *The Clocks of Columbus*, pp.202, 209.

20 Thurber, "The Catbird Seat," in *The Thurber Carnival*, pp.9–14. The British made a wonderful film based on "The Catbird Seat," titled *The Battle of the Sexes*, in 1959. It starred Peter Sellers, Robert Morley, and Constance Cummings. See Holmes, *The Clocks of Columbus*, p.251.

21 Holmes, *The Clocks of Columbus*, p.321.

22 John Mortimer, "Insomniac's Companion," in Holmes, *Thurber*, p.153.

23 Bernstein, *Thurber*, p.387.

24 Letter to Herman Miller, May 28, 1943, quoted in Bernstein, *Thurber*, pp.352–53. "That Thurber Woman," *Newsweek*, Nov. 22, 1943.

25 Bernstein, *Thurber*, p.355.

26 Peter De Vries, "James Thurber: The Comic Prufrock," in Holmes, ed., *Critical Essays*, pp.37–38.

27 Thurber, "The Wizard of Chitenago," in *The Wizard of Oz* (Greenwich, Conn.: Crest, 1960), pp.vii–viii.

28 Bernstein, *Thurber*, p.365.

29 Holmes, *The Clocks of Columbus*, p.310.

30 Holmes, *The Clocks of Columbus*, p.228; letter to Herman and Dorothy Miller, Dec. 9, 1944, quoted in Bernstein, *Thurber*, p.367.

31 Dan Nortin, *New York Times Book Review*, Feb. 4, 1945, quoted in Holmes, *The Clocks of Columbus*, p.244.

32 Letter to E. B. White, June 9, 1943, quoted in Holmes, *The Clocks of Columbus*, p.243.

33 Kenney, *Thurber's Anatomy of Confusion*, p.8.

34 C. Lester Walker, "The Legendary Mr. Thurber," *Ladies' Home Journal*, July 1946, quoted in Bernstein, *Thurber*, pp.369–70.

35 Thurber, introduction to *The Thurber Carnival*, p.xiii; Bernstein, *Thurber*, p.375.

36 Holmes, *The Clocks of Columbus,* p.233.

37 Bernstein, *Thurber,* p.373.

38 Thurber, "Our New Natural History," in *The Beast in Me,* pp.151–66; see also Black, *His Masquerades,* pp.102–3.

39 Thurber, "The Olden Time," in *Beast in Me,* pp.283–86.

40 Letter to E. Louise Malley, Jan. 7, 1945, quoted in Bernstein, *Thurber,* p.372.

41 Rosemary Thurber, interview with author, Mar. 28, 1992.

42 Letters to Sarah B. Whitaker, 1947–1949, printed in "James Thurber on the Perplexities of Educating a Daughter," *Chicago Tribune Magazine,* May 2, 1963. See also Holmes, *The Clocks of Columbus,* pp.252–53.

43 Letter to Dr. Gordon Bruce, Jan. 9, 1946, quoted in Bernstein, *Thurber,* p.384.

44 Cooke, "James Thurber in Conversation with Alistair Cooke," *Atlantic,* Aug. 1956, p.39; Bernstein, *Thurber,* pp.385, 388; Holmes, *The Clocks of Columbus,* p.223.

45 Bernstein, *Thurber,* pp.385–86. *Life,* Mar. 14, 1960, pp.104–5, photo by Tibor Hirsch.

46 George Plimpton and Max Steele, "James Thurber," in Fensch, ed., *Conversations,* p.61; "The Secret Distractions of James Thurber," *Hartford Courant Magazine,* Aug. 30, 1959.

47 Holmes, *The Clocks of Columbus,* pp.255–56.

48 Letter to attorney Alexander Lindey, Apr. 4, 1949, quoted in Bernstein, *Thurber,* pp.393–94.

49 *Time,* July 9, 1951, p.88; see Holmes, *The Clocks of Columbus,* p.289.

Chapter 6

1 Thurber, Ohioana Medal speech, quoted in Holmes, *The Clocks of Columbus,* p.273.

2 John Fullen, letter to Thurber, Jan. 31, 1946, quoted in Bernstein, *Thurber,* p.389.

3 Letter to the editor of the *New York Herald Tribune,* Dec. 3, 1947, quoted in Bernstein, *Thurber,* p.390; Holmes, *The Clocks of Columbus,* p.262.

4 Letter to Dorothy Canfield Fisher, Apr. 11, 1951, quoted in Bernstein, *Thurber,* p.410.

5 Interview with Henry Brandon, *The New Republic,* May 26, 1958, collected in Fensch, ed., *Conversations,* p.104.

6 U.S. Department of Justice, Federal Bureau of Investigation file on James Grover Thurber, obtained by the author through the Freedom of Information Act (FOIA), Request No. 360,514, submitted Apr. 29, 1992, reply issued June 15, 1993.

7 "Writers Organize to Fight 'Censors,'" *New York Times,* Feb. 25, 1948; California Legislature, Fourth Report of the Senate Fact-Finding Committee on Un-American Activities, 1948, Communist Front Organizations.

8 Barnard Rubin, "Broadway Beat," *The Daily Worker,* Sept. 30, 1947.

9 Brandon interview, pp.104–5; interview with Harvey Breit, *New York Times,* June 29, 1952, in *Conversations,* p.32.

10 Thurber, "Dark Suspicions," *The New York Times,* July 27, 1952, extracted in Bernstein, *Thurber,* p.410.

11 Thurber, *The 13 Clocks,* p.120. See Bernstein, *Thurber,* p.405; Holmes, *The Clocks of Columbus,* p.263.

12 Bernstein, *Thurber,* p.66.

13 Thurber, *The 13 Clocks,* p.73. See Kenney, *Thurber's Anatomy of Confusion,* pp.155–57.

14 Thurber, introduction to *The 13 Clocks,* quoted in Bernstein, *Thurber,* p.405.

15 Letter to Dr. Russell Voorhees, Mar. 3, 1951, in Bernstein, *Thurber,* p.405; letter to Joel and Gertrude Sayers, Dec. 13, 1950, in Thurber and Weeks, eds., *Selected Letters,* p.185.

16 Plimpton and Steele, "James Thurber," in Fensch, ed., *Conversations*, p.62. See Bernstein, *Thurber*, p.406; Holmes, *The Clocks of Columbus*, p.267.

17 Bernstein, *Thurber*, pp.412–13.

18 Letter to E. B. and Katharine White, July 10, 1951, reprinted in Bernstein, *Thurber*, p.414.

19 Bernstein, *Thurber*, p.415; *Time*, July 9, 1951, p.89.

20 Letter to Carey McWilliams, Aug. 13, 1952; letter to E. B. White, Apr. 25, 1952, both in Bernstein, *Thurber*, pp.416–17.

21 Letter to Ronald Williams, Dec. 15, 1951, quoted in Bernstein, *Thurber*, p.419.

22 Letter to Ohio State President Howard L. Bevis, Dec. 6, 1951, in Bernstein, *Thurber*, p.422.

23 Letter to Lester Getzloe, Oct. 26, 1951, in Bernstein, *Thurber*, p.421.

24 Bernstein, *Thurber*, p.424.

25 Letter to Ronald and Jane Williams, Nov. 11, 1952, in Bernstein, *Thurber*, pp.426–27; letter to Peter De Vries, Oct. 16, 1952, in Bernstein, p.430; letter to John McNulty, undated, in Bernstein, p.431.

26 Letter to Ronald and Jane Williams, Mar. 14, 1953, in Bernstein, *Thurber*, p.434.

27 Thurber, "Do You Want to Make Something of It?" quoted in Holmes, *The Clocks of Columbus*, p.285.

28 Thurber, "Make Something of It," quoted in Holmes, *The Clocks of Columbus*, p.285.

29 Thurber, "The Duchess and the Bugs," Ohioana Sesquicentennial Career Medal speech, in *Lanterns and Lances*, pp.176–77.

30 Ohioana speech, cited in Holmes, *The Clocks of Columbus*, p.3.

31 Letter to George Smallsreed, Sept. 23, 1953, in Bernstein, *Thurber*, p.440.

32 Bernstein, *Thurber*, p.183.

33 Letter to Malcolm Cowley, Jan. 18, 1957, in Bernstein, *Thurber*, p.444.

34 Holmes, *The Clocks of Columbus*, pp.292–93.

35 Letter to Frederick Sauers, Jan. 5, 1954, quoted in Bernstein, *Thurber,* p.441.

36 Kenney, *Anatomy of Confusion,* p.182.

37 Thurber, "The Truth About Toads," quoted in Holmes, *The Clocks of Columbus,* p.296.

38 Bernstein, *Thurber,* p.448.

39 Holmes, *The Clocks of Columbus,* p.279.

40 Peter De Vries, introduction to Thurber's *Lanterns and Lances,* reprinted in Holmes, *Thurber,* pp.162–64.

41 "Up With a Chuckle, Down with a Yuk," *Newsweek,* Feb. 4, 1957.

42 Red Smith, "Jim Thurber," *New York Herald Tribune,* Nov. 3, 1961, cited in Holmes, *The Clocks of Columbus,* p.279.

43 Interview with the Associated Press, Aug. 27, 1961, in Holmes, *The Clocks of Columbus,* p.310.

44 "Mr. Thurber Gives Advice to Women," interview with Virginia Haufe, *Ohioana,* Summer 1960, collected in Fensch, ed., *Conversations,* p.85.

45 Kenney, *Anatomy of Confusion,* pp.167–71.

46 William L. Shirer, *A Native's Return,* p.203.

47 Letter to William Maxwell, Oct. 11, 1956, in Bernstein, *Thurber,* p.449.

48 Interview with Henry Brandon, in Fensch, ed., *Conversations,* pp.107–8.

49 Letter to Fred Allen, Sept. 3, 1954, in Bernstein, *Thurber,* p.458.

50 Letter to E. B. White, July 26, 1957, in Bernstein, *Thurber,* p.458. Maurice Dolbier, "A Sunday Afternoon with Mr. Thurber," *New York Herald Tribune,* Nov. 3, 1957, in Bernstein, *Thurber,* p.459.

51 Thurber, *The Years with Ross,* pp.47, 75, 79, 80, 92.

52 Thurber, *The Years with Ross,* pp.149, 144, 137.

53 Thurber, *The Years with Ross,* p.137.

54 Groucho Marx, letter to Thurber, June 3, 1959; Thurber, letter to E. B. White, Dec. 3, 1958; both in Bernstein, *Thurber,* p.462.

55 Letter to Edmund Wilson, May 19, 1959, quoted in Bernstein, *Thurber,*

p.464; Heywood Hale Broun, interview with author, July 24, 1991.

56 Philip Hamburger, interview with author, Nov. 24, 1991.

57 Thurber, *The Years with Ross*, p.77.

58 Roger Angell, interview with author, Feb. 10, 1992.

59 Bernstein, *Thurber*, p.463; Linda H. Davis, *Onward and Upward: A Biography of Katharine S. White*, pp.179–80.

60 Letter to E. B. White, Dec. 3, 1958, in Bernstein, *Thurber*, p.462.

61 Bernstein, *Thurber*, p.463.

62 David Thomas, letter to author, Dec. 20, 1991.

63 Holmes, *The Clocks of Columbus*, p.313; Bernstein, *Thurber*, p.470.

64 Edmund Wilson, *Upstate*, p.221, cited in Bernstein, *Thurber*, p.470.

65 Ann Buchwald, conversation with author, Apr. 4, 1992; Bernstein, *Thurber*, p.452.

66 John Updike, "Writers I Have Met," *The New York Times Book Review*, Aug. 11, 1968.

67 Angell interview.

68 Rosemary Thurber, interview with author, Mar. 28, 1992.

69 Bernstein, *Thurber*, pp.452, 475.

70 Letter to Edmund Wilson, May 25, 1959, in Bernstein, *Thurber*, pp.455–56.

Chapter 7

1 Bernstein, *Thurber*, p.472; Holmes, *The Clocks of Columbus*, p.322.

2 Bernstein, *Thurber*, p.472; Holmes, *The Clocks of Columbus*, p.322.

3 Holmes, *The Clocks of Columbus*, p.312.

4 Bernstein, *Thurber*, pp.472–73.

5 Bernstein, *Thurber*, p.477.

6 Thurber, "The Thurber Method of Acting," *New York Times Magazine*, Oct. 16, 1960, p.28.

7 Letter to Ronald and Jane Williams, fall 1960, quoted in Bernstein, *Thurber*, p.478.

8 Bernstein, *Thurber*, pp.479–80.

9 Letter to Bernard Hollowood, editor of *Punch*, Mar. 8, 1961, quoted in Bernstein, *Thurber*, p.489.

10 Thurber, foreword to *Lanterns and Lances*, p.xv.

11 Elliott Nugent, *Events Leading Up to the Comedy*, p.302, quoted in Bernstein, *Thurber*, pp.474, 484.

12 Letter to Roger Angell, July 3, 1961, in Bernstein, *Thurber*, p.484.

13 Roger Angell, interview with author, Feb. 10, 1992.

14 Angell interview.

15 Angell interview.

16 Bernstein, *Thurber*, p.488.

17 Letter to John Gude, Feb. 25, 1961, in Bernstein, *Thurber*, p.488.

18 Letter to E. B. White, June 19, 1961, in Bernstein, *Thurber*, pp.489, 491.

19 Edmund Wilson, *Upstate*, pp.222–23, cited in Bernstein, *Thurber*, p.493.

20 Bernstein, *Thurber*, pp.495–97.

21 Bernstein, *Thurber*, pp.499–500.

22 Bernstein, *Thurber*, pp.501–2.

23 Bernstein, *Thurber*, p.502.

24 Letter to Mark Van Doren, Nov. 12, 1959, quoted in Bernstein, *Thurber*, p.503.

25 E. B. White, "James Thurber," *The New Yorker*, Nov. 11, 1961.

26 White, "James Thurber."

Portfolio

1 Letter to Frances Glennon, June 30, 1959, in Thurber and Weeks, eds., *Selected Letters*, p.123.

2 Rosemary Thurber, interview with author, Mar. 28, 1992.

3 Thurber, *Men, Women and Dogs*, pp.169–80.

4 Interview with Henry Brandon, *The New Republic*, May 26, 1958, reprinted in Fensch, ed., *Conversations*, p.102.

5 Brandon interview, p.97.

6 Brandon interview, p.97.

7 John Halperin, conversation with author, February 1992.

8 Dorothy Parker, introduction to *Men, Women and Dogs*, pp.vii–x; Thurber, *The Beast in Me*, p.73.

9 Letter to Barbara Kammer, Mar. 5, 1945, quoted in Bernstein, *Thurber*, p.183.

10 Rosemary Thurber interview.

11 Interview with W. J. Weatherby, *Manchester Guardian*, Feb. 2, 1961, reprinted in Fensch, ed. *Conversations*, p.87.

12 Holmes, *The Clocks of Columbus*, p.134.

Chapter 8

1 Russell Baker, "He Knew When to Stop," *The New York Times*, Apr. 12, 1990.

2 Tim Warren, "Garrison Keillor Looks at Guys with Wit, Wisdom, Wistfulness," *The Baltimore Sun*, Nov. 14, 1993.

3 John Updike, letter to author, Jan. 8, 1992; *Hugging the Shore* (New York: Alfred Knopf, 1983), pp.839–40.

4 Updike, *Hugging the Shore*, pp.839–40.

5 Updike, letter to author.

6 Stephen A. Black, *James Thurber: His Masquerades*, pp.7–8.

7 Samuel Bernard Baker, "James Thurber: The Columbus Years," master's thesis cited in Kenney, *Thurber's Anatomy of Confusion*, p.3. Thurber interview with W. J. Weatherby, *Manchester Guardian*, Feb. 2, 1961, collected in Fensch, ed., *Conversations*, pp.86–88; quoted in Holmes, *The Clocks of Columbus*, p.328.

8 Letter to E. B. White, Apr. 24, 1951, in Bernstein, *Thurber*, p.237; "The Case for Comedy," *Lanterns and Lances*, p.142.

9 Eastman, *The Enjoyment of Laughter*, p.342; Kenney, *Anatomy of Confusion*, p.174.

10 Thurber, introduction to *My Life and Hard Times*, quoted in Kenney, *Anatomy of Confusion*, p.174.

11 Kenney, *Anatomy of Confusion*, p.4.

12 Thurber, "The Quality of Mirth," *New York Times*, Feb. 21, 1960.

13 Kenney, *Anatomy of Confusion*, p.5.

14 Weatherby interview, p.87; see Holmes, *The Clocks of Columbus*, pp.196, 328.

15 Interview with the British Broadcasting Corporation, Dec. 24, 1958, cited in Holmes, *The Clocks of Columbus*, p.221.

16 Tony Kornheiser, *The Washington Post*, Nov. 24, 1991, in Bernstein, *Thurber*, pp.236–37.

17 Interview with Judd Arnett, *Detroit Free Press*, Jan. 12, 1960, pp.15–16, in Fensch, ed., *Conversations*, p.75; interview with Harvey Breit, *The New York Times*, Dec. 4, 1949, in *Conversations*, p.16.

18 From *Thurber on Humor* (Cleveland: World Publishing, n.d.), p.10; see Kenney, *Anatomy of Confusion*, pp.71–72.

19 Breit interview, p.16.

20 Interview with Henry Brandon, *The New Republic*, May 26, 1958, in Fensch, ed., *Conversations*, pp.101–2.

21 *Time*, July 9, 1951, p.95; interview with Lewis Gannet, *Harper's Bazaar*, Nov. 1950, in Fensch, ed., *Conversations*, p.24.

22 See Kenney, *Anatomy of Confusion*, p.121.

23 Weatherby interview, p.87; Brandon interview, p.110.

24 Thurber, *Let Your Mind Alone!*, pp.57–65; see Holmes, *The Clocks of Columbus*, pp.195, 197; Kenney, *Anatomy of Confusion*, p.30.

25 Letter to E. B. White, Sept. 30–Oct. 5, 1943, in Holmes, *The Clocks of Columbus*, p.241.

26 Thurber, *Let Your Mind Alone!*, cited in Holmes, *The Clocks of Columbus*, pp.186, 201; Kenney, *Anatomy of Confusion*, pp.37–38.

27 Letter to E. B. White, Jan. 20, 1938, in Holmes, *The Clocks of Columbus*, p.187; letter to Malcolm Cowley, July 3, 1951, in *The Clocks of Columbus*, p.270.

28 Thurber, *Bermudian*, Jan. 1951, in Holmes, *The Clocks of Columbus*, p.14.

29 See Holmes, *The Clocks of Columbus*, pp.30, 51, 106, 126.

30 Holmes, *The Clocks of Columbus*, p.253.

31 Holmes, *The Clocks of Columbus*, p.253. Plimpton and Steele, "James Thurber," in Fensch, ed., *Conversations*, pp.59–60.

32 Letter to Herman Miller, Sept. 27, 1931, in Holmes, *The Clocks of Columbus*, p.125.

33 Undated letter to John McNulty, in Holmes, *The Clocks of Columbus*, p.111.

34 Undated letter to Herman Miller, in Holmes, *The Clocks of Columbus*, p.133.

35 Thurber, "The Lady on the Bookcase," in *The Beast in Me*.

36 Dorothy Parker, "Unbaked Cookies," collected in Holmes, ed., *Thurber*, p.56.

37 Brandon interview, pp.98–99.

38 Thurber, *Beast in Me*, p.74.

39 Brandon interview, p.99; Holmes, *The Clocks of Columbus*, p.144; Robert E. Morsberger, *James Thurber*, p.164.

40 Cooke, "James Thurber in Conversation with Alistair Cooke," *Atlantic*, Aug. 1956, pp.36–37; "Thurber and His Humor," interview with *Newsweek*, Feb. 4, 1957, pp.52–56; in Holmes, *The Clocks of Columbus*, p.229.

41 Edmund Wilson, *The New Yorker*, Oct. 27, 1945; see Black, *His Masquerades*, p.103.

42 Richard C. Tobias, *The Art of James Thurber* (Athens: Ohio University

Press, 1969), chapter 7; Holmes, *The Clocks of Columbus,* pp.231–32. See also Kenney, *Anatomy of Confusion,* p.112.

43 E. B. White, undated letter, in Holmes, *The Clocks of Columbus,* p.237.

44 Kenney, *Anatomy of Confusion,* p.191.

45 John Updike, review of *Credos and Curios, New York Times,* Nov. 25, 1962, quoted in Holmes, *The Clocks of Columbus,* pp.303–4.

46 Kenney, *Anatomy of Confusion,* p.18; Updike, review of *Credos and Curios.*

47 "How to Tell Government from Show Business," in Michael J. Rosen, ed., *Collecting Himself: James Thurber on Writing and Writers,* p.231; Thurber, "Carpe Noctem, If You Can," *Credos and Curios,* p.98.

48 "The State of Humor in the States," *New York Times,* Sept. 4, 1960.

49 *New York Times,* Apr. 16, 1959, in Rosen, ed., *Collecting Himself,* p.222.

50 Eastman, *Enjoyment of Laughter,* p.341; Plimpton and Steele, "James Thurber," *Conversation,* p.63. See also Bernstein, *Thurber,* p.237.

51 Rosen, ed., *Collecting Himself,* p.218.

52 Helen Thurber, introduction to *Credos and Curios,* p.x.

53 Interview with Rod Norell, *Christian Science Monitor,* June 4, 1959, in *Conversations,* p.67.

54 Kenney, *Anatomy of Confusion,* p.4.

55 "This Petty Pace," *Credos and Curios,* p.30.

56 "E.B.W.," *Credos and Curios,* p.136.

57 "The Incomparable Mr. Benchley," *Credos and Curios,* p.150.

Bibliography

Anyone who writes about James Thurber is indebted to the research and insights of those who have undertaken in the past to delve into his life and work. Chief among these sources are the exhaustively thorough 1975 biography by Burton Bernstein, of *The New Yorker* staff, and the 1972 literary biography by Charles S. Holmes. In recent years, the 1984 study by Catherine McGehee Kenney builds impressively upon the foundation established by Robert E. Morsberger in 1964 with the first analysis of Thurber's writings, and Stephen A. Black's fine 1970 contribution to the study of Thurber's works.

Bernstein, Burton. *Thurber: A Biography.* New York: Dodd, Mead, 1975.

Black, Stephen A. *James Thurber: His Masquerades.* The Hague: Mouton, 1970.

Davis, Linda H. *Onward and Upward: A Biography of Katharine S. White.* New York: Harper & Row, 1987.

Eastman, Max. *The Enjoyment of Laughter.* New York: Simon and Schuster, 1936.

Fensch, Thomas, ed. *Conversations with James Thurber.* Jackson and London: University Press of Mississippi, 1989.

Holmes, Charles S. *The Clocks of Columbus: The Literary Career of James Thurber.* New York: Atheneum, 1972.

———, ed. *Thurber: A Collection of Critical Essays.* Englewood Cliffs, N.J.: Prentice-Hall, 1974.

Kenney, Catherine McGehee. *Thurber's Anatomy of Confusion*. Hamden, Conn.: Archon, 1984.

Lopresti, Robert, ed. *Thurber on Crime*. New York: Mysterious Press, 1991.

Morsberger, Robert E. *James Thurber*. New York: Twayne, 1964.

Rosen, Michael J., ed. *Collecting Himself: James Thurber on Writing and Writers, Humor and Himself*. New York: Harper & Row, 1989.

Shirer, William L. *Twentieth-Century Journey: A Native's Return, 1945–1988*. Boston: Little, Brown, 1990.

———. *Twentieth-Century Journey: The Start, 1904–1930*. Boston: Little, Brown, 1976.

Thurber, Helen, and Edward Weeks, eds. *Selected Letters of James Thurber*. Boston: Little, Brown, 1981.

White, E. B., and Katharine S. White, eds. *A Subtreasury of American Humor*. New York: Coward-McCann, 1941.

Books by James Thurber

Is Sex Necessary? or Why You Feel the Way You Do (written with E. B. White). New York: Harper and Brothers, 1929.

The Owl in the Attic and Other Perplexities. New York: Harper and Brothers, 1931.

The Seal in the Bedroom and Other Predicaments. New York: Harper and Brothers, 1932.

My Life and Hard Times. New York: Harper and Brothers, 1933.

The Middle-Aged Man on the Flying Trapeze. New York: Harper and Brothers, 1935.

Let Your Mind Alone! and Other More or Less Inspirational Pieces. New York: Harper and Brothers, 1937.

Cream of Thurber. London: Hamish Hamilton, 1939.

The Last Flower. New York: Harper and Brothers, 1939.

The Male Animal (Co-author Elliott Nugent). New York: Random House, 1940.

Fables for Our Time and Famous Poems Illustrated. New York: Harper and Brothers, 1940.

My World – and Welcome to It. New York: Harcourt, Brace, 1942.

Many Moons. New York: Harcourt, Braçe, 1943.

Men, Women and Dogs. New York: Harcourt, Brace, 1943.

The Great Quillow. New York: Harcourt, Brace, 1944.

The Thurber Carnival. New York: Harper and Brothers, 1945.

The White Deer. New York: Harcourt, Brace, 1945.

The Beast in Me and Other Animals. New York: Harcourt, Brace, 1948.

The 13 Clocks. New York: Simon and Schuster, 1950.

The Thurber Album. New York: Simon and Schuster, 1952.

Thurber Country. New York: Simon and Schuster, 1953.

Thurber's Dogs. New York: Simon and Schuster, 1955.

A Thurber Garland. London: Hamish Hamilton, 1955.

Further Fables for Our Time. New York: Simon and Schuster, 1956.

The Wonderful O. New York: Simon and Schuster, 1957.

Alarms and Diversions. New York: Harper and Brothers, 1957.

The Years with Ross. Boston and Toronto: Atlantic, Little, Brown, 1959.

Lanterns and Lances. New York: Harper and Brothers, 1961.

A Thurber Carnival (play). New York: Samuel French, Inc., 1962.

Credos and Curios. New York: Harper & Row, 1962 (posthumous).

Thurber and Company. New York: Harper & Row, 1966 (posthumous).

Index

39–41, 42, 56–59; on *The New Yorker*, 124–25; as performer, 21, 136; personal relations, 38–39, 50–53, 60, 96, 122, 131–32; and Harold Ross, 33, 113–14; and school, 7–8, 8–9, 76, 83, 123; and Strollers Club and Scarlet Mask Club, 18, 20, 23, 135; travel, 17–18, 23–27, 64, 67–70, 78–82, 83, 119–20, 130–31, 140–41. *See also* animals; battle of the sexes; comic strips; drawings by; FBI file on; humor; language; Manley, Jared L.; Mok-Mok; Monroe stories; "Notes and Comment"; Ohio State University; tragicomedy; women; word games; *and names of individuals and titles of individual works*
Thurber, Leander, 3
Thurber, Mary Agnes (Mame), 2–3, 85, 111, 113, 121, 151
Thurber, Robert, 5, 11, 18, 70, 111–12, 115, 130
Thurber, Rosemary, xiii, 20n., 49–50, 56–57, 65, 80, 98, 116, 132, 143, 145, 147, 148
Thurber, William Fisher, 4–6, 8, 11, 70–71, 77, 111, 112–13
Thurber Album, The, 111–13, 132
Thurber Carnival, A, 134–37, 140–41, 153, Thurber's appearance in, 136
Thurber Carnival, The, 95–96
Thurber Country, 116, 167
Thurber's Dogs, 120
Tierney, Gene, 82
Time, 99, 102

" 'Tip, Tip Hurray!' The Battle Cry of Greedom," 28
Tobias, Richard, 162
Toklas, Alice B., 55
tragicomedy, Thurber on, 154
"Truth About Toads, The," 121
Tunney, Gene, 126
Twain, Mark (Samuel L. Clemens), xvi, 95–96, 130, 139, 153
Tynan, Kenneth, 130

"Unicorn in the Garden, The," 73, 135
"University Days," 11
Updike, John, xiii, 131–32, 150–52, 164

Valentino, Rudolph, 28
Van Doren, Carl, 107
Van Doren, Mark, 79, 88, 89, 137
Vanzetti, Bartolomeo, 79
Veeck, Bill, 84
Victor Emanuel, 85
Vidor, King, 81
Von Kuegelge, Elfride (Fritzi), 137

Ward, Artemus, 96
Warren, Tim, 151
"Waters of the Moon, The," 102
Weekes, Hobart, 51, 128
Wells, H. G., 68
West, Rebecca, 98, 130
"What a Lovely Generalization!" 101
"What Do You Mean It *Was* Brillig?" 71–72, 155
"Where Are They Now?" series, 63–64